O Death, Where Is Thy Sting?

O Death, Where Is Thy Sting?

A Meditation on Suffering

Joe Hoover

ORBIS BOOKS

Maryknoll, New York 10545

Founded in 1970, Orbis Books endeavors to publish works that enlighten the mind, nourish the spirit, and challenge the conscience. The publishing arm of the Maryknoll Fathers and Brothers, Orbis seeks to explore the global dimensions of the Christian faith and mission, to invite dialogue with diverse cultures and religious traditions, and to serve the cause of reconciliation and peace. The books published reflect the views of their authors and do not represent the official position of the Maryknoll Society. To learn more about Orbis Books, please visit our website at www.orbisbooks.com.

Library of Congress Cataloging-in-Publication Data

Names: Hoover, Joe (Chaplain) author.
Title: O death, where is thy sting? : a meditation on suffering / Joe
   Hoover.
Description: Maryknoll, New York : Orbis Books, 2020.
Identifiers: LCCN 2020022218 (print) | LCCN 2020022219 (ebook) | ISBN
   9781626983922 (trade paperback) | ISBN 9781608338566 (ebook)
Subjects: LCSH: Suffering—Religious aspects—Christianity. |
   Death—Religious aspects—Christianity. | God
   (Christianity)—Omnipresence.
Classification: LCC BV4909 .H66 2020 (print) | LCC BV4909 (ebook) | DDC
   248.8/6—dc23
LC record available at https://lccn.loc.gov/2020022218
LC ebook record available at https://lccn.loc.gov/2020022219

A.M.D.G.

Contents

The Glory of God

F OR A FEW WEEKS AS A NOVICE I was a chaplain in a gray jail for kids. I think of it as gray because the boys wore gray sweats and the walls were cinderblock and the air was dead and the quiet unnatural and I did not want to be there. I wanted the boys to not be there, too. I prayed with them, insisted on the learning of lessons. Three-point plans, step by little step, sure-fire methods—biblical and secular—for staying out of trouble and away from the Minneapolis JDC.

Over the weeks, one of the guards, Paul, had been watching me. Finally, he told me something that stopped me cold. "Every one of these kids," he said, "will be back. Every one." These kids will be in and out of jail, and back in again. Some for the rest of their lives.

This guard was not trying to be gloomy. He was just stating what is. He had worked at this place for twenty years. He was telling me what he knows. All these inmates, nearly all of them black children, will get out of here and live their lives and go back to the streets and then end up, again, back in juvy; eventually, many of them will end up in state or county or federal prison for months or years, maybe for life. There is no hope for those kids. Their souls? Sure. Lives as free men? No. End of story. Thirteen-year-old boys headed to life in a cage.

Why were they born? For this? Is anyone born for prison? Evidently some are. And others are born for, who knows, endless soccer camps that parley a half-hearted midfielder onto first-team All-Metro. Neither party asked for their state in life. It just happened. Two were grinding at the mill, one was taken away, the other left to breathe the fresh clean air.

Is there a God? A ridiculous question. We all know the answer to that. Just look around. Behold: we are so far past the Beginning and yet the earth is still a formless wasteland, darkness covers the abyss of us, a ferocious wind sweeps over foul waters and these children are going away forever.

No matter what we do, no matter the counseling, the stern but loving discipline, the schooling, the life-training —Do they even receive such things?—they will all be back.

The guard wore a black sport shirt. He came across like a reasonable-minded school counselor, one who might lean forward in a leather chair and quietly nod his head every so often as a kid tells him about his mom's charming, violent boyfriend. His black hair was not feathered, but it may have been several years back. The boys were segmented into groups, lived in pods, tucked into cells with heavy doors and thick glass. He said it calmly. They will return. All of them.

Is there a God? An even worse answer: There is a God and every one of those kids is coming back.

Who or what can we blame for this? Society? The breakdown of the family? The obliteration of father figures? A lack of jobs, the pervasiveness of drugs, crowded schools, harsh drug laws, the proliferation of guns, the profit-seeking prison industry, brutal cops, institutional racism, corrupted civil will, a deflation of things spiritual in the general culture? Religious novices and their ignorance of the absurd rates of black incarceration? Simply the twelve-year-olds themselves?

Why doesn't God, who has lovingly given us free will, take it back for a few minutes? Take it back and airlift these children into a life of excellent schools, churches that bring the gospel to the streets, cities abundant with jobs, and just make things better? It is too discouraging. The bad has been so lodged into, so caked over the world, evil become so stuck, with old growth and tree rings and roots reaching way down, so much sadness that it will take ages to chip it away.

Oh, maybe if we all just believe in Jesus Christ enough he will blast through and save us. Like children at a *Peter Pan* matinee reviving Tinkerbell, if we keep clapping and clapping and clapping our hands, Christ will appear and briskly lift us out of these tragedies. Is that how it is? Is it? An act of will can upend the whole rotten thing? Heresy, you say? Trying to force God onto the scene? Are we simply to wait? Wait to make sense of sadness, of evil? Then, as we wait, don't we begin to feel a little stupid?

"I'm waiting, it's coming. Just hang on. It'll all get better."

"Good for you! How adorable. He's waiting, the dear. He really thinks it will all get better."

"God is good!" some religious person says, as if she is saying, "Panama is an isthmus." Who says such things so matter-of-factly? God is good? Where do you live? God is good! Said by the same people who think they are going to win Powerball every time they buy a ticket. God is good?

These days are an exciting time for New Atheists, and I wonder, who is not a new atheist? Who does not pass into the cold? We all wish for something as clear and convincing as science to bind up all wounds, heal every ill, patch up all rents in the existential fabric. So that nothing ever goes down again.

I STOOD ON MY ROOF on the Lower East Side and watched the second tower fall. Its crumbling and falling felt like the most unreal and the most solidly real thing I had ever seen. It was as if the falling were a kind of creation. A collapsing of concrete and mass and purpose and will so resolute and final that it seemed in its very nature to be a new thing. It went down in a cascade of gray and black powder, and I expected some kind of mystical spirit shadow to remain there, because how could nothing be there? But there was no such consolation for a distant viewer.

Instantly, it seemed, the names and faces of the missing appeared taped to lampposts, street signs, bus stops and subway walls. Their faces stared out as their families asked, "Have you seen this person? Where is this man, this woman? Call this number if you have seen her."

It was also as if the dead were staring out and asking us, the living, *Where are you? Who are you? This is not a joke. We really are missing. Why are you still walking around while we have vanished into vapor? What gives you the right? The right to be on the living side of this smudged, torn, and godforsaken flyer while we languish among the disappeared?*

And far, far away, as all the numbers click in the right slots, God is good!

GOD IS GOOD? God is just?

I met Philip and we prayed together in his room. We crouched down on the floor and looked at his candles and a rocket he had drawn and pictures of his dead brother, Aaron, the archangel Michael, Jesus, a priest named Henri. These icons sat in his prayer corner, a cardboard box covered with a red bandana; somehow Philip had found me worthy to help him worship here.

When we prayed, Philip, who was in his fifties, talked to his brother Aaron, who himself could never talk, as if Aaron were right there. Philip said to Aaron, "You are in my heart," and he meant it. As if Aaron were, literally, a tiny man abiding in Philips's aorta. He also said to Aaron, every time, "You gotta help me."

I wondered if Philip said this because his mind was ravaged by illness, because he was hunched over when he walked, and he couldn't speak very fast, or eat very fast, or get anywhere fast. Because every single solitary morning, Philip hated waking up.

If Philip was in his room and needed someone, he put his fingers in his mouth to whistle but instead a yell came out. Or, if he fell off his bed while trying to get his clothes on, he would shout, "Somebody come and help me!" Sometimes he stumbled when he walked into a room, and with the precious bravado of a child sitcom actor he would mutter, "Some days you just can't win." One day he said to me, "You are in my heart." I froze, and stopped breathing.

PHILIP LIVED outside Toronto with a cluster of people like him in homes with those who assisted them. It was called L'Arche Daybreak. I was there as one who had just finished the Spiritual Exercises of St. Ignatius of Loyola. I came cresting on a spiritual wave. Sometimes I looked around and couldn't help but feel how beautiful and spiritual it must be to live as one of these weak, vulnerable, and honest people who talk directly to the dead; who yell happily when they mean to whistle; who make loud, moaning noises in church because they have no control over their bodies and voices. How holy and blessed are these wounded people. Here at L'Arche, the flood waters were baptismal, everything anointed.

Nevertheless, even if all that happened at L'Arche was holy, it was disturbing to consider the pain of being anointed like that. Maybe those back-pew moans were not delightful. Maybe they were moans arising from the horror of being engulfed and drowned and helpless to do anything about it because you just don't have it in you. Being at the mercy of people like me who come and go for six weeks, six months, a year at a time. Being taken care of, all the time, day in and day out. Being always a burden, always suffering.

Maybe that is why Philip watched Batman movies, put on Superman t-shirts, slept in Spiderman pajamas. To clothe himself in powers alien to his body. There he was, stumbling around with that big red "S" on his chest, and it all felt like a cruel joke.

THE BITTER JOKE that we fall for every time is that God created us to be greatly depleted so that we could become abundant in God. The Lord cast us deep into the well of mean existence so we would grasp onto the rope he throws down. We rely on God to get us through the terrible things God lets happen to us.

It's all a set-up. Like giving a child five cents when admission to the fair is twice that. The child has to come back for the extra nickel, and to get past the gate again he has to come back again, and keep coming back, and back, and back, and has to be grateful, oh so grateful, this kid, to the Keeper of the Coin!

The fix is in, and has been basically forever. God made us sick so we would reach out to the physician in him. I boast of my weakness, says Paul, for when I am weak then I am strong, for the Lord is strong in me. I boast of my obliterated face on the subway wall, my body trapped in a tiny cell. I brag that I hate getting up in the morning, that when I use the toilet, I need someone to wipe for me. God made us frail so that God could swoop in and be mighty for us, and how needy, self-involved, and completely screwed up is that?

WHY IS IT THIS WAY? It is the child's most basic question, dealing with the most bewildering thing of all. Referring to life and its diamond-sharp edges, harsh enough to throw us down at a moment's notice, all overseen by a God whose love, coiled up in the cells of our cells, firing every moment of our existence, evidently drives people into the ground on a daily basis. Why?

This question rears up again and again in our lives. Who gets the healthy genes and why? Why does one financial analyst have to jump from the seventieth floor while another walks away in a dust-covered suit? Behold any crumbling human sputtering and begging on the sidewalk: There but for the grace of God....

Really? The shining thread of God's grace was held out to you and not to him? And he received from the Lord what? A sharp stick in the eye?

Sometimes the goodness of God, the order of the universe, and the joy of any given life appears to be a tightrope made of braided grass: it could disintegrate at any moment.

How come? We can look around at the created world, we who inhabit it as poorly as we do, and we can ask: Who thought any of this was a good idea? It may be, we are told, that the planet is careening toward irreversible catastrophe. Who let this happen? Is it something that can even occur? Can we really blow it, utterly and entirely, the energy of us collapsing the entire gift of creation? And if so, is it really our fault? Weren't we all just trying to drive to church?

It matters little, I think, that these eternal questions wind through the life of a Catholic religious, a Jesuit sent from this place to that, plains reservations to humming cities, El Mozote to a small, dark-lit chapel, and points between. Any soul paying the barest attention to life gasps, at least now and then, at the apparent ludicrousness of it all, no?

The glory of God, says St. Irenaeus, is the human being fully alive. And any human fully alive can get shattered by life again and again. Which leads to the question: When will God get enough glory that we can quit being so completely alive and just sit around for a few minutes?

Merry Sunshine

MERRY SUNSHINE'S PLACE was about the size of a Volkswagen bus with a high ceiling. It was populated with the dogs King Henry the Eighth and Sunshine, the cat Molly, a foul-mouthed parrot named Cava de Costa. We sat in the kitchen where a radio tuned to a local station powered entirely by the sun sent us Bob Dylan—*You've got a lotta nerve, to say you are my friend*—his bitter words coming off, somehow, lighter here.

In the room next door slept a man named Thomas. "My gentleman," Merry said more than once. I suspected new love. Thomas was recovering from any number of things—booze, an old bike wreck, sleeping in the pines for months. Merry checked on him every so often while she cooked and pointed out where things were in the apartment. I just kind of sat there quietly and watched. Merry's unkempt hair, the way it framed her face, reminded me of a lion. A calm, peaceful lion; somewhat detached.

Merry lived in Taos, brought food to the poor, and took in wandering strangers like me. I was on a month-long pilgrimage from our St. Paul novitiate, needed a place to stay, and was directed to her house. Merry did not hover over me busily, inquiring after my tastes, my past, or my health. Her hospitality was not oppressive. A couple of times, it almost seemed like she forgot I was there. She just did what just was doing. And I don't know if there was an onion skin's difference between what she was doing and who she was. I sat at the kitchen table breathing the quiet air, gnawing on chicken, and liking, improbably, every song that played over the sun's radio.

Merry told me she used to live in upstate New York and, after a divorce and a bad car accident that left her with a permanently injured back, she decided to overhaul things entirely. She went to a workshop at a friend's church where she held her palms up and breathed deep for thirty minutes while asking God a question. Later, in a dream, she saw mountains and a river. A few days after that, she saw a photo with the same mountains and river. It was a picture of Taos. The message, to her, was clear: Go to that place and feed people. So she did.

The mountains in the picture were the Sangre de Cristo—the blood of Christ. What a holy thing to drink from.

When I woke up at Merry's place the next morning, she trundled Thomas and me out to a church to stand in line for free food. We loaded bags with turnips, carrots, loaves of bread, pasta, meat, chocolate, tiny juice boxes, and a raft of other groceries for ourselves and whoever else might come along.

Merry and I went to the hospital and visited a veteran named Red Eagle afflicted with mono and maybe TB, his lungs crammed, he told us, with black guck that he'd been coughing up all day. Merry was happy about this progress and encouraged him to keep coughing.

We went to the forest and took food to a small gathering of Rainbow Nation kids camped out there. They strolled the woods with authority, cooked and cleaned in a tidy kitchen of sticks and dried mud, yelled "I love you!" to each other through the twilight. A few just sat in a wrecked car and drank. One of the Rainbow kids came back with us to spend the night, along with two or three drunk older men. Later, at Merry's door appeared a young couple in tie-dye (on their way to a Phish concert? I can't exactly remember) who had heard of this kind lady. They eagerly came inside, flushed and hungry. None of this made Merry nervous or overwhelmed. She just made more chicken. She fed us all, and then we collapsed to her floor for the night and the dogs squeezed in where they could.

"So, where you gonna go now?" Merry asked the next day. It was mid-morning and everyone else had already left. Clearly, I wasn't being invited to stay a third day. As I packed up my stuff, Merry and Thomas gave me tips, kind of impatiently, even though I hadn't asked, on begging, dumpster diving, and hitchhiking. Merry laid her hands on a speckled blue metal cup and gave it to me for the rest of my journey.

She decided to give me a little black skillet, too. Then her own gray fleece. She ended up giving me sweatpants, mittens, a scarf, a towel, a can of Sterno, a roll of toilet paper, matches, candles, a sleeping bag, a pink and teal ski jacket, a pair of women's jeans, and four-days' worth of food. As I walked out the door, she found, somewhere, a medal that said, Mary, Our Lady of the Roses. She put it in my palm and said to keep in touch. It felt meant. I don't think Merry said probably four words in a week that she didn't mean.

It had snowed as we slept, and I walked away from her apartment past trees and bushes crystallized with ice, glinting in the morning sun. An impossible silvery wonderland; bright, cool, suspicious. Things aren't really this way. You don't really meet someone like Merry, someone who sends you off in a shimmery landscape like this. I had entered a different place, somewhere out of the known boundaries. How else to explain it? Had I tried to go back, the tear in the fabric would have sealed up and all would have vanished.

After I had completed my pilgrimage and returned to St. Paul, I wrote Merry a letter to thank her. Nine months later I got a letter back.

She had lost my letter with my address, then found it half a year later on the dash of her broken pickup. The mechanic had had the truck for five months, but had never fixed it. A lot of things like this had happened to

Merry Sunshine since I left. She was no longer able to make rent on the apartment and moved out. She was house sitting in a cabin even smaller than her old place. It had no electricity, no phone, no outhouse, only a wood stove for cooking and heat. I was prepared to hear she had put a halt to her Dorothy Day routine—feeding the hungry, welcoming the stranger—and was just trying to survive. She wrote:

> *I've been chopping wood and have not been cooking for people. The cabin is 1/2 mi. off the main Road no one visits. I have been Really busy hitchhiking almost every day into Taos to get the food bank going. Fri the computer lists comes in from the Santa Fe food bank of which Sunshine Foundation is a member. Taos County Food Bank is the official name with the IRS for my agency for the foodbank. Sat or Sun I walk (if no one picks me up) about 8 miles up the hill and back (4 each way) to confer with the gent who helps distribute. Mon I hitchhike into town and fax the order. Wed I line up someone with a Truck to pick up Thurs. delivery. Thurs I hike in to accept delivery—Sometimes it comes on Fri. Then I help load truck and we drive 29 miles to deliver it. Next week do it all again.*

It was enough to care for total strangers at her own place. But this! She had mentioned something about a food bank and a Sunshine Foundation, but it just seemed to me like wishful thinking. Of course she's starting a food bank. What else would she be doing? I stare at her words—blue ink crammed onto every inch of perhaps the only clean white sheet of paper she owned—and, as if it's a living thing, I ask the letter: What is going on here? What insane love brings all of this to bear? Did all the mercy in northern New Mexico get concentrated into one tall woman with an ax and little else? Or could it be that she is merely one of those people who can't sit still? Maybe she's just a drone-ish, task-oriented person who needs to fill her days, that's all.

How is she this way, and why? The gift of a car wreck and a damaged back? Those thirty minutes when she held her palms in the air? Some terrible light from the pure emptiness of the universe that took her soul and placed it right inside the souls of broken human beings everywhere? Just what has gotten into this woman?

Remember Thomas? He lived with me at the time you visited (and gave you the sleeping bag). We all called him Bird or Birdman because he has the parrot. I have been dating him since April—went to see him in Santa Fe where he moved in May to see a specialist about his seizures caused by a motorcycle crash (20 yrs ago). I went to see him Thanksgiving. He was very shy wondering if I still cared. My messages were not given to him by the manager of his

handicapped housing. I called 12 times. He re-
ceived 2 messages. My letters came back. At
Christmas we passed each other by a half hour.
He went to Taos I went to Santa Fe. We don't
have phones or cars. Ride given by friends. I
ended up camping in the Gila Wilderness with
some friends of friends. He was told I died along
the road in Arizona and called the mental health
hotline 3 times at pay phones in front of grocery
store. Manager called police as he was drunk.
He's in jail with 3 assaults against officers. So
Thomas needs our prayers....

The poverty that can so easily lead to charity—Who more than anyone else tends to the poor? Other poor people. The prisoner? Other prisoners.—had veered into one of its tragic byways. I hear this story and I see people wandering in the dark. An absolute dark in a burnt-out wasteland, hearing all around them, on the outskirts, the buzzing and clicking and ringing of all the things everyone else has and they do not. We don't have phones or cars. Prophetic and hopeless. We don't have...to miss each other by a half hour. We don't...and he's in a parking lot drunk and freaked out, convinced she's dead. We...and he's in jail.

Merry seems to embrace the poverty she's been given. She doesn't get bitter about it, she lives gracefully through it, and life gets harder anyway. She throws her energy into a makeshift foundation that has to recreate its donor base every other day in the form of whoever picks her up hitchhiking; she feeds all the poor people that she can scrounge up; she simply tries to love a man and write him and be with him and, in the end, she is ignored and passed by and presumed dead.

Maybe, in spite of all her unflagging resolve, drinking from the Sangre de Cristo doesn't feel redemptive for Merry. Maybe, sometimes, it only seems like more spilled blood. She gets no prizes, only more chaos. Those that have little, even that will be taken away from them.

Sorrowful Mysteries

I N THE WINTER, the war was always there and we did not go to it because we were Jesuits thinking and praying and reading, and sometimes it was Hemingway we read. In the evenings, snow fell over Chicago and it clumped between the slats of the benches outside the classrooms where every old idea was overturned only to find there was nothing new beneath. It was a cold winter and the wind came in off the lake.

That winter, a few of us got together on the third anniversary of the invasion of Iraq—just before Lent began—and prayed a rosary on the street near the lake. The idea was that we would all wear our clerics, our black outfits, and hold signs. It would be a mighty thing for drivers to see all these religious people in black praying and demonstrating against the Iraq War. It's an image, we felt, people hadn't seen so much.

But it was so cold and so windy out that most of us had on jackets that covered up our black shirts and small white collars. There was no impressive black line. Just a bunch of people in winter coats, beige and green, red and gray.

We stood out there anyway. We prayed. We held signs and prayed the Sorrowful Mysteries, even though it was Monday, the day you pray the Joyful Mysteries. A few nuns and a few undergrads joined us. There were about twenty of us: Jesuit scholastics, a few of the priests, and these others, lifting from Friday the Sorrowful Mysteries, the Passion, and announcing them on Monday. "Hail Mary, blessed be your womb, the hour of our death."

What did it accomplish? What did it matter? A few of us kept doing it, on Fridays. It felt strange. We recited the Sorrowful Mysteries on the appropriate days, Fridays in Lent, strangely.

On one of the Fridays, it rained. Whoever was in charge of the signs didn't bring them. He thought they would get ruined. Because there were no signs, I didn't want to pray the rosary that day. The people of Chicago driving by Loyola would have no clear idea why we were out there praying. We couldn't be doing this to them; out there, giving confusing signals to sleepy morning drivers. We prayed anyway. "O good Jesus save us from the fires of hell, lead all souls to heaven, especially those in most need of thy mercy."

What was this? Why were we there? How did we mess up? Who left behind the signs to tell the world what we were doing?

Our signs for peace, when it wasn't raining, said to the people of Chicago, "Peace is our duty, our grave duty." And "War is always a defeat for humanity." Two quotes from our recently departed pope. Another sign said, "Lord have mercy on us." We made these simple signs and we held them and we recited the ancient prayers.

But, really, who were we to hold signs while saying prayers? Isn't it over, the solemn clutching of cardboard posters? Aren't we, in this era, through with it? Haven't we entered a time when this is so primitive and lonely and nonsensical, a sparse row of earnest spiritualists holding signs and praying to end war? Why drag ourselves back a few decades to this kind of thing? Holding a sign, on a street, with traffic going by. It's presumptuous to think that the people out there need to hear our message. It is too righteous by half. It borders on haughty.

And there we were, in our blacks, feeling at turns ghostly, fraudulent, simplistic, not doing near enough, too little too late, and not entirely convinced this was hopeless. We wanted, at least, to do something.

A few months before we prayed the rosary on the street, Dan Berrigan came to our school. He was invited to deliver a talk about—of all things—art. In the middle of wartime, Fr. Daniel Berrigan, SJ, came all the way to Chicago, to Loyola, to speak about a painting! A Caravaggio painting, Christ betrayed by Judas. He read a paper about what he felt this painting meant, and we all listened respectfully and wished the paper was about disobedience and war. We wished he would gather us up, Fr. Berrigan, and take us to Catonsville, where we would all non-violently burn something up. We would perform an act that, in some small but searing and generation-defining way, might affect the continuance of the war.

He did not do that. He talked about this painting of Christ in Gethsemane, soldiers taking him away, and a man in the corner painted by Caravaggio to look like Caravaggio; the genius painter as one of the mob, holding a lantern that lights up his own face. The artist addressing his own guilt, Fr. Berrigan speculated. Caravaggio once killed a man, he told us, and this painting somehow spoke to that. Murdering another man, for Caravaggio, was somehow like being an accomplice in killing Christ.

Caravaggio wanted to shine a light on himself as one who helped betray the Lord. One who in his own way never did enough to stop the crucifixion; who would paint himself as standing by stupidly—a witness to a horrible wrong—in order to scourge some harsh and unredeemed bone in his body.

After Fr. Berrigan spoke, I went up and introduced myself. I shook his hand and said soberly, "I am a Jesuit."

He looked up a bit more brightly when I said that. Maybe he has practiced looking up brightly when young men shake his hand and tell him they too are Jesuits. He wore a green and brown and orange shirt. It looked somewhat like camouflage. I tried to find some significance in this. I wondered for a moment whether Dan Berrigan was wearing a shirt like that with the wily intent of reclaiming camouflage from the military, of putting it on his own peaceable body and thereby disarming camouflage. Maybe he just liked the shirt. He said in this shirt to the whole crowd, after he had stopped talking about art and we asked him about war, that these past four years had been the most difficult of his life.

The most difficult of his life! Dan Berrigan! Has he even been to jail at all these past four years? The toughest of his life! After all he's been through. Fugitive from the FBI, years in jail, reviled for speaking out against abortion, or in favor of Palestine. These last four years the hardest of his life!

It's not how one's life should go! Shouldn't you, Daniel, be dealing with injustice in a way that makes your life, though *challenging*, as all of our lives are *challenging*, at least wear on your body a little more gently? Shouldn't you, while yet disturbed by war, find a slot to put it into, one that doesn't shake you so deeply? Haven't you already stood before these wars, witnessed what humans can do to one another, felt imprinted in your flesh the helplessness of trying to do good in a corrupt world?

You are in your eighties! Your ninth decade shouldn't be like this. Stop it! Quit being so beset. We insist. Cut it out!

We would all like to be undisturbed when we are eighty-four-year-olds. We all want to be, in a beautiful and smart way, always on the correct side of issues like war. But who wants any of that to make their life too difficult? Good-hearted Christians want to be free. In Jesus, they say, is freedom. If we keep getting closer to Jesus there will be great freedom. Even the cross we will take on with greater ease at that age, without so much pain and maybe even with joy. The cross won't hurt as much when we are so close to Jesus after decades of diligent practice.

These have been the toughest four years of my life. Is the more one cares about the world the more miserable one becomes? Is there a deeper struggle that must be taken on—opening the soul to a dissatisfaction, an unease that will leave one never quite at home in the world, always taken down into grief by the violence going on out there? Shall we be sent back into the desert with Merry Sunshine, flailing around to help the poor? What exactly is the call? Is standing on the corner holding the words of a dead holy Polish actor enough?

The war continued. Another year came and went. Eighty thousand Iraqi civilians gone, the population dropping daily. Some weeks after the fourth anniversary of the war's start, students from Loyola decided to visit

Senator Barack Obama's Chicago office. A vote was pending to allocate money for an increase in troops and a general continuation of the war. These students wanted the newly elected senator to vote against it. A few Jesuits joined them. We would bring to Obama's office a poster, with signatures and handprints of other students and messages about peace.

We knew the senator wouldn't be there, we just wanted to speak to someone. We took the train and rehearsed our arguments. When we got there, we showed our poster, made our case. Obama's polite staff told us they were not sure what the senator, now the presidential candidate, would do about the upcoming vote. It was very complex.

One thing was sure, Obama was a uniter. He would try to unite people around this or any other issue. But as for how he would vote, they could not say. The staff would nevertheless convey our feelings to the senator. We left and gathered in the lobby. We tried to say upbeat things, the kinds of things people who petition the government say to each other. The good of our just having gone there... every little voice... you just never know. We said these things to each other and wondered if we really believed them. Maybe we were little drops of water forming a river. And maybe that river would... do something.

It so happened that, not long after this, Fr. Berrigan came back to our college to receive an honorary doctorate.

Before the ceremony, he spoke in an informal session with students. This time, it was mainly about war and civil disobedience and prayer. He was funny and humble and down to earth. We asked him, "How do you do it, how do you keep going, how do you struggle for peace?"

He answered with the fairly simple things that a religious person might say. He told us that he reads the Bible. He prays with a community. He is less and less concerned with results. He said that he invites students to protests with him. He will stand by any student who gets arrested with him. He will stand with them before the judge, or before their families. He will be there for them, he said matter-of-factly.

"How did his life as a Jesuit influence his work?" I asked. He said that, after Ignatius's conversion, he walked through Spain and laid down his sword before the Black Madonna in Manresa.

After answering a number of questions about war and jail and so on, he said something like, "Now that I've completely depressed you all..." and everyone laughed.

Fr. Berrigan also had on the same shirt. The same orange, green, brown, nearly-but-not-quite-camouflage shirt he'd worn at the Caravaggio talk. I tried again to find some significance in this. I tried to connect it to the last time he was at our school. I wondered if this was the shirt he wore to all talks on peace and war and art. Or had he worn only that shirt for the past two years? Or since the war began? I did not know.

Maybe he was just a guy with a lucky shirt. A ballplayer on a hitting streak—superstition and a whiff of sentimentality. Were these still the hardest years of Berrigan's life? I couldn't tell. He seemed in good spirits, but that didn't necessarily mean things had gotten easier for him.

Barack Obama actually did wind up voting against funding the surge. Did our little drops of water help create the river of his vote? Was it a thing caught up in prayer, spirituality, the eternal? Or was it just a candidate getting himself on the right side of an issue? Or are those two motivations not so distinct? Who can say exactly? But others voted for it, and the surge was funded anyway. Eventually it was credited with helping to bring a modicum of peace to Iraq. Maybe we were wrong. We were wrong and the mantra of the regime in *1984* was right, War is Peace.

Then Obama became president and funded his own surge, and eventually the war in Iraq ended, but really it didn't end, it just shifted, mutated, reconfigured, rose up in new factions and fresh brutalities, and, in one way or another, it still goes on and War is, basically, War.

At the end of his conversation with us, Fr. Berrigan said that recently he had been on a retreat in New Mexico with Catholic Workers. They are people who try to carry out the corporal works of mercy and witness for peace. The theme of this retreat was "Walking with Our Sorrows." They too, apparently, lifted those mysteries from Friday and used them for other days. Father Berrigan told us he liked that theme very much, that we are walking with our sorrows.

OH THE SORROWS. The sorrows of life! They show up everywhere. A man speaking to a woman at a coffee shop in a college town in Northern California.

– Do you want to go to a cheese tasting with me?

– Where?

– At the women's faculty club.

– Is there a men's faculty club?

– No. There's just the faculty club and a women's faculty club. I just thought I'd see if you wanted to go.

– Well, uh, I'm lactose intolerant.

– I understand. My son is lactose intolerant.

– I can't eat a lot of cheese.

– You know, they have cheeses these days that don't have lactose in them...

– Oh. Right.

– ...but I can't guarantee that all the cheeses

there would be lactose free. Still, they will
have other foods.

– Yes. Well, you should go. It will be nice.

– Yeah, I just thought I'd see if you wanted to
go.

You hurt just listening to this conversation; your
soul is cracked. You want to fix them both. Why such
disconnection! How long will this man be asking women
to wine and cheese events at, strangely enough, the
women's faculty club, until one of them says yes? How
long, O Lord, how long until we see thy face? What is
thy face that we might see it? When will the world be
made comprehensible for us? When will you lift us out
of our human poverty? Or is that the point of human
poverty?

I AM NOT in this little spiritual volume trying to tell anyone what to do or how to think. (Says everyone about to
tell you what to do or how to think.) But I will tell you
this about being a Christian. Or just being created. This
is one of the fundamentals that gets drilled into you. It's
in two parts.

1. You don't deserve any piece of your precious
   little life. It is all the free gift of a God who

really doesn't have to do anything at all for you. Not a single blessed thing; and,

2. You are virtually the reason God exists. God, in all his merciful and towering might, does nothing but dote on the tender lamb of you all day and all night.

To recap:
You are nothing.
You are everything.

Some wise person tells you the first part, another the second. A third person tells you both in the same breath: "You, my child, are loved unconditionally, so roam the earth as if all its lovely offerings were fit gently into place for you. Each one is a chance for you to delight in, because each moment is a divine chorus of love and praise for you."

And (same breath) "Sink, wretch, to thy knees hourly for mercy from the divine presence, because you draw every whisper of breath only at his behest, who by the raising of a single eyebrow could crush you at any moment."

And once you think you have it, the balance—the shuddering humility, let us call it, of knowing you are loved unconditionally by a God who doesn't have to love you unconditionally—you don't have it. According to Jacques Derrida, a splendid atheist, perhaps, who may as well be speaking for all believers: everything that has been said must be unsaid. Don't fix too tightly on what you think you know. Things have a way of turning, real quick.

So, should Merry Sunshine expect the bounty of the Lord for all her works of mercy? Or ought she be grateful that she at least has a heart to feel things? Should Philip at L'Arche demand that the Lord do far better for his neural pathways because the world is created for him? Or is his only option to be outrageously grateful that the Lord Almighty has given him at least this much health?

We deserve everything and we deserve nothing. What more can be said?

Passion

THE LIFE, DEATH, AND RESURRECTION of Jesus Christ, we are told, is the only way to make sense of tragedy, war, any kind of unspeakable suffering. His death is a more extraordinary event than his birth—more powerful, for my money, than his resurrection. Down through the eons, gods have entered the world. They are born into this earth and they do great things, or terrible things—they are god-like. But have any of them let themselves be killed? To suffer so terribly? Your ordinary average deity can enter the world as a giddy rutting swan . . . but to let himself get taken down! Taken down, and hard. This is, let's say, unique.

The Jesus in our childhood wood-grain-brown Stations of the Cross pamphlets had no face. Jesus's face was just a blank space of beige. Why no eyes, no mouth, no nose, no face? To unsettle us? Is it symbolic? Is it to signify that our faces are meant to be there? That we are

Christ somehow? Why no face? Something is profoundly wrong with Jesus.

Why the gloom? The stomach-churning blank-faced Jesus? Is it because the gloom and sadness will come anyway, so we might as well stop and worship it? To claim for the church that unlovely appellation "misery" before someone else tacks it on us? To get in front of, so to speak, the news cycle? To own the story before it owns us?

Nor did the soldiers have faces. Are we the soldiers killing Christ? Nor did the women weeping and wailing have faces. (If they do this in the green wood what will they do when it is dry? Oh, Jesus, there is nothing but dry wood around here!)

Why are we so fixed on death? Consider the Stations of Light. Have you heard of such a thing? In the Catholic Church? Stations of Light? They are real! Oh that these could become as popular as the dispiriting ones! The Stations of Light have been around for thirty-some years. After two thousand years of spears and nails, we finally got around to celebrating the resurrection! Mary Magdalene runs to tell the others. Hearts are burning on the road. Fingers in wounds. Fish by the sea. Feed my lambs.

So, why don't we wayward souls kneel solemnly before Magdalene turning and seeing the risen Lord camouflaged as a gardener? Why don't we bow before Peter and John rushing to the tomb?

Could it be because these resurrection stories are not so dramatic and baroque? Death and the foreclaws of tragedy are always more captivating for the artist than life and joy. Or could it be because death is just so overwhelming that it sucks up any attention we might give to life?

The world is fallen. Well, who let it fall? Upon what flimsy shelf was the world laid? What splintered crutch did it lean its weight on? Mistakes were made. A fall happened. The passive voice of governmental denial. Events of descending took place. And who is responsible? Why don't they show their face? We are told it was Adam and Eve whose "original sin" kicked off this path. Their "pride," their attempt to be like God led to the sin that led to the sins that led to the sins, and so on down to the packed jails in Minnesota and the depleted firehouses in New York and the girls sold in South Asian alleyways, cash on the barrelhead.

But really? Blaming Adam and Eve? Two grasping people set all this in motion? Augustine considers it so, that it was all Adam and Eve's fault, but was he correct? Or was he just trying to explain away his own sins?

Perhaps our murky questions of God's absence are simply a matter of low self-esteem. How could the king love such a louse as me? A scarcity mentality—a fear that that there is not enough compassion to go around, that God has scattered, he has scrammed. He is not at work behind the scenes. A staging of *Macbeth*, where we are not sure whether Macduff really is going to stroll in from the wings and slay the insatiable king. We don't believe in the hero because we are just prosaically pessimistic by nature. A sad disposition clouds our view of the holy one! So mundane, our motives! The eternal questions of God's presence cratered in mere psychology.

These questions. Aren't they a little self-involved? A bit *modern*? Tragic things shouldn't happen to us! We shouldn't be so sad! Because we are at the limit, the flush edge of history. We are all Teilhard de Chardin traveling toward the Omega point, the final reconciliation of all things. It is all getting better, so we shouldn't suffer so much. Pestilence is outdated. Disease shouldn't so swiftly take us down. We are the people who can manage our lives better than anyone else ever could! The latest date that human time has ever reached is right now! This present is the living future of all futures that ever existed. No one has ever gone farther than right here and right now. We should have advanced well beyond such miseries!

When did we start asking these questions, these totalizing, awful questions: "Why is there suffering?" "Where is God when we crash and burn?"

Suffering just is, right? For centuries, and centuries, it just happened and everyone got it. They understood. People lived, they died; things went terribly wrong, and *unfairly*. But humans didn't have a need for things to be completely unsullied, for the living of life to be perfected, did they? They were closer to the dirt, nearer to the life of death and the death of life. Oh, isn't it so contemporary and well-fed and Western of us to be angry at God, bewildered by God, denying of God. The choice to become an agnostic or atheist is perhaps a privilege only the well-heeled can afford.

Untimely death and suffering in the poor reaches of the planet is just a thing that happens because no one is special and no one, as they say, gets out alive. Way back, many children died at birth, or at age one or two or three, it was like losing a vase. Before the modern era, about a quarter of all children died in their first year of life; almost half before they reached age fifteen.

Sad, tragic, devastating maybe. But was God hauled up to the witness stand every time a six-month-old never woke up? Probably not. You grieved, you moved on. But now it is apparently different. We expect to be treated better.

"The world is full of infidelity," cries out Jean Pierre de Caussade. "How unworthy are its thoughts of God! It complains continually of the divine action in a way that it would not dare use toward the lowest workman about his trade."

The French Jesuit upbraids humanity: "We are surprised at the treatment endured by Jesus Christ at the hands of the Jews, but, O divine love! Adorable will! Infallible truth! In what way are you treated?"

And: "My good souls! Nothing is wanting to you. If you only knew what these events really are that you call misfortunes . . . you would be deeply ashamed and excuse yourselves of your complainings of blasphemies."

He is in the same territory as the old priest in Flannery O'Connor's "The Enduring Chill." Asbury, dramatically dying, though he probably isn't, wants an intellectual conversation with a clergyman—preferably some inscrutable Jesuit—about James Joyce, about art as prayer. Instead, he gets at his beside a loud, half-blind parish priest. "Do you want to suffer the pain of loss for all eternity? How can the Holy Ghost fill your soul when it's full of trash? The Holy Ghost will not come until you see yourself as you are—a lazy ignorant conceited youth!"

We are horrid people, all of us. There, it has been said. Doesn't it feel good to name it? And maybe it is only in the capturing of the creature under the glass—the indecent, sinful thing of us—and calming it down and looking at it and naming it for what it is that we can ever hope to claim anything better.

"There has never been a generation of men and women," says Annie Dillard, "who have lived well for even a day." Because the sin at the depth of all our souls threatens to overwhelm us every minute of our life. Sin is lurking at your door, Cain, its urge is toward you. Not just when the fruit of your ground has been rejected by the Lord, but every minute you're alive.

In Francisco Zeffirelli's *Jesus of Nazareth*, Pilate asks the Jews which one he should release—Barabbas or Jesus. Stirred up by the chief priests and the elders, the crowd bays for the release of Barabbas, while Mary tries to get them to release her son.

"Jesus!" Mary shouts from the courtyard beneath the parapet. "Jesus!" as she is pushed about and stifled by the crowd. If only those people on the "Release" side had yelled hard enough! They might have won his freedom and he would not have been crucified and died. If only! We could have avoided this! It was in the realm of possibility, no?

As I child I watched this with pain. Every nail shall be counted, every wound shall be cataloged, every shove of the Virgin be filmed. Zeffirelli and Scorsese, Pasolini and Gibson, and any given Renaissance painter. The Catholic Church like some crack squad of crime fighters chalking bodies and detailing every trace of blood. It all has been measured. We worship death, no? We glory in suffering! We look at it over and over again, a Zapruder film of Christ's passion that we can't get enough of. Tammy, a Protestant, once told me her church doesn't have the body of Christ on their cross. Because he's not on that cross anymore, she said. He's resurrected. They just have the two boards.

Pause. Long pause.

I'd never thought of that! Of course! He's resurrected! Why do we have him on that cross? We have it all wrong. We should be like Tammy's church. We should just have the two boards! That makes so much sense! Take him off. He's risen!

Why all this focus on the dead Jesus? Everything so somber, the ceremonies of torture, the gleaming blood of the cross. All those grim, forbidding churches: Holy Agony, Our Lady of Sorrows, Five Holy Wounds, and resting behind glass in Turin: the Shroud of Turin. The Duccio print hanging in my room, Mary in a deep blue habit gravely holding her newborn, already mourning, while the numinous little man of him in orange gown and gray cloak pushes away her veil, perhaps comforting her because of what lies ahead. An infant who is consoling his mother because he is soon going to rip her heart out of her body. He was born, you could say, to destroy this woman, for at least a while, and he knows it. The Metropolitan Museum of Art bought this painting for $45 million. It is eleven inches tall.

THE PAINFUL BLASTING HUMANITY of Christ. We place ourselves before it as Duccio once did. Christ! What do we do with this one? How much can we take? So much there, even as a child. His voice was free, as with all children. As an adult, the same: emotionally liberated, unblocked, limber, no vocal tension. He can rise and thunder, like that, like Lee Cobb in *On the Waterfront*: speaking quietly, then a roar, and then back down again. Jesus soft and low: *Tonight one of you will betray me*...then full throated: *All of you will abandon me!* Rising up, standing, pointing a wavering finger like a drunk man, but speaking without bitterness, without even condemnation or accusation, if that is possible given such accusing words, but just naming truth. Unbidden, the truth rises up: shadowed room, fire in sconces, stone dishes and cups, the tactless voice, not waiting for the right moment but just pouring itself out. Hamlet. O God, this too, too solid flesh will be pierced...epileptic fits of melancholy, determination, rage. He stands up, points, you will all . . . pauses, stops himself. *Let's drink.* The response: *We will not abandon you!*

You are weak, he fires back, but somehow without harshness, for they cannot take harshness. *Weak!* A coach naming truth that a team can hear only as love because of the way the coach is. Truth, said a recent pope, is love.

No, says Christ to the apostles. *I apologize. You're just human. Come, let us drink!* And they drink, not out of fear of some mad king but because they want to. They love him, he loves them, and they know it. Like a great actor, the sudden movements on this appalling night, the dark sky oddly clear, and him seized in his wild moments, primitive nature, overcome with emotions, letting himself be carried, letting himself go as the spirit will take, feeling every feeling.

This is the one we conform ourselves to. We put our suffering into his. Is it enough? Can we trust that pitching all in with Jesus is enough? Oh, isn't he a lot? Difficult to be with? Christ? A bit much? An exposed nerve of a man? Someone you can take only for so long, all that unvarnished humanity? Does he bear not only his future pain but the wounds, words, deeds, and things of all, for all time: the splitting of the atom, the finding of fire, the exploding of the bomb, the child pinned under the Pinto, the dog sunk in a black pond, the smoke rising over the vain city, the first split cell, mutation of fish, arrow into the beast, tufts of gun smoke, sunspots on a high window, gallons of cold coffee. Does he bear it all, Christ, churning within him, every war that ever was or ever will be, dancing in his molecules so that it is just challenging to be around this man? Does Christ carry the you of two thousand years away, you and all your petty madness, the girl you left behind, the bad movies, the failed exams, the love child, the weird quiet relief of cutting the lawn; the crushed cathedral, the mushroom and the cloud and the way a snake turns everything around it into sacred fear? Does he bear that, him down on the end of your bench? Is this just a bit much to be around? Can one so simple and plain as he is, *no majestic bearing to catch our eye*, heft all and everything of the world? All the food and all the insects and all the disease. The disease, love, joy, tender flesh in a battlefield; a carjacking, a first kiss, a last breath. Does he carry these things, he who became sin? Where do you fit within him? And upon which shelf shall you put him? He who was tempted in all ways except sin, did he do that *for you*? Jesus, is he everyone's digits, the ends of your hairs, the wife not your own, the ruler you shudder at, the bitter end of the appendix, the severed breast, the sexless nights, the common snapdragon, the Council of Trent, the Battle of Hastings, the pill, the eyelash he brushed away, St. Irenaeus, St. Isidore the Farmer, fruits and grains, minerals and elements, sodium and ruthenium, birds and wildfire, glaciers and disappeared glaciers, every couplet of Shakespeare's and each child's drowning nightmare—does he contain them all, things lovely or horrifying, his body bursting at the seams, so hard to live with it. (He's fully human after all! And his divine nature does not steal away hurt from his human nature; the God of him does not swoop down and siphon pain from the Man he is. I have my theology correct, no?) Is this him, all of everything stuffed inside? How does one bear such a man as this?

AND THE "PASSIVITY OF GOD." God not "making" anything bad happen, God not "the cause" of suffering. Thomas Aquinas tells us God merely allows evil to bring out the good.

But isn't one percent of divine passivity basically one thousand percent God doing it? If the almighty God of the universe lets a thing happen, then he is for all intents and purposes making it happen. A leader of an armed battalion filing his nails while down the hill yonder a massacre gets underway. The colonel is complicit. Bad men need nothing more to compass their ends, a latter-day John Stuart Mill might say, than that good gods should look on and do nothing.

A mother watches her child walk for the first time. She knows she has to let him fall or he will never learn to walk. It's the difficult thing a mother has to do—to let the kid crash; to let the child uncomfortably go through the frightening moments so he can get over them.

But this same mother does not let her son *cheerfully stroll into traffic*. She lets the boy fall on the ground, *on the carpet*, but she doesn't "allow" him to get hit by a car.

What father would give his child a snake when he asks for a fish, or a stone when he asks for bread? I can think of one. We are given stones all the time. (Or, they just passively roll off the Father's mantle, these stones, while he shrugs, "I didn't make it happen.")

Has God never said, *I am responsible for your pain?* Has God never indicted himself? God who clasps his hands behind his back and refuses to step in and take care of us. God who ontologically changes a seminarian who as a priest changes the ontology of a woman he kicks out of the confessional; orders her out for telling him what she'd done as a frightened girl years back, leaving her shame unreleased, deepened, entrenched. This really happened.

What do we do with this? At what remove is God behind any suffering, large or small? Nothing is just us and just chance. Why should his power and majesty preclude the power and majesty it takes to be worthy of the accusation of Primary Cause of Great Suffering?

The loving laissez faire of God's economy brings his people to the woodshed again and again and again, and he knows it and he wonders if he just didn't make it all too hard.

WHEN IT CAME TO DIVIDING things up, how did Hades get the underworld while Zeus received the sky and Poseidon the sea? Hades drew the wrong lot. One chance out of three and he gets hell.

And you, do you ever wonder what slim scrap of paper you blindly chose? How it came about that you were cast for a day, a year, a decade into your own underworld? An abyss that, like Hades, eventually becomes so identified with you that it gets named after you, if only by the tricks of your own mind? I have spent the past five years in the depths of Brian. I'm sunk in the trenches of Terrell. Surely I am going straight to Kaitlyn, if I am not already there.

Something came down, everyone else got sea and air and you got the dark lower passages, and what do you do?

And it is true, speaking of lower depths, that after the towers fell and men were held in chains at black sites in total darkness with neither food nor water while music blared at insanely high volumes for weeks at a time in order to break their wills and squeeze out information, not only did that music include violent rap and heavy metal, but also on the playlist were children's songs, and jingles. The "I Love You" song by Barney and Friends, and the "Meow Mix" theme were played over and over again, a thousand decibels high. Anything can be turned into a weapon. *Guantanamo's Mixtape*, Scott Bruce called it, the "soundtrack of Hell."

"Cursed be Canaan!" cried Noah. "A servant of servants shall he be unto his brethren." Fifteen words that have been used down through the ages, in a way having to do with Noah's son Ham, to justify black slavery. And when a Bible justifies a thing, that thing is hard to get unjustified. It tends to stick.

Then, eons later, in the 1960s, the scholar Gerhard Von Rad comes along and points out, in a way having to do with a "later redactor," that this Genesis narrative originally said nothing about Ham. The story does not justify this servitude.

So, do we lay blame for the atrocious centuries of black slavery at the feet of one biblical redactor? One man who inserted into the original story that Ham was the father of Canaan? And if that is true, why did it take the universe so long—until the middle of the twentieth century!—to deliver unto us Professor Von Rad to clear all this up for us?

Many other things have been used to justify black slavery. But this passage does seem to have pride of place. And had it been de-fanged way back when...?

On the fifteenth anniversary of the Iraq War, Iraqi filmmaker Sinan Antoon pointed out that the perpetrators of that human catastrophe are still at large, yet even to be tried in court. "A year ago, I watched Mr. Bush on *The Ellen DeGeneres Show*, dancing and talking about his paintings." Should he be? In *Esquire* magazine that same week, Charles Pierce asserted that the former president should be in stocks.

And if that is true, if George W. Bush should not be cavorting on a daytime talk show but wasting away in his own black site, how is the world's air even breathable that he isn't? How do we even wake up in the morning when this outrage continues? Why is the earth not spontaneously combusting every minute the ex-president and all those who delivered us into Iraq are out there on the lam, and not even pursued?

Death row inmates have been known to declare they never would have got right with God unless they had known they were soon going to die. Thomas Aquinas, the angelic doctor, says that, indeed, the death penalty is a gift to them. "The death inflicted by the judge profits the sinner, if he be converted, unto the expiation of his crime."

And so it would seem that those who advocate for the use of the death penalty are shadow spiritual directors, providing these doomed men an avenue toward peace with the divine.

Nagasaki was incinerated by the atomic bomb only because the city of Kokura was obscured by clouds. Droplets of water and dust congealed in the sky to divert a horrific weapon over to our unsuspecting village and render you untouched.

Aquinas considers in the *Summa Theologiae* whether it is the case that the blessed rejoice in the punishment of the wicked. He quickly and sanely objects to the question, saying that rejoicing in another's evil pertains to hatred. And hatred is not a Christian value. Then Aquinas answers his own objection, and this is the final word. It is okay, he writes, for those in heaven to look upon those in hell and be glad.

"The saints will rejoice in the punishment of the wicked by considering the order of divine justice, and their own deliverance, which will fill them with joy."

If that seems a touch horrifying, let us not kid ourselves. Who doesn't sometimes silently rejoice when they are rewarded for their virtue while others around them pay for their transgressions?

In his book *Police Craft*, a cop named Adam Plantinga tells of the time when, in a pitch-dark backyard, he confronted a suspect who may have been wielding a knife and may have just killed his wife. The man got up off the ground and started walking toward Plantinga. "As far as I knew...he was coming to kill me too. Shoot that guy and the community calls you a cold-blooded murderer. Don't shoot, and now maybe you have a knife lodged in your neck and your wife is raising your two daughters alone."

(He split the difference and knocked down the guy with his gun.)

The point of all these vignettes? I'm not sure if such confounding, mind-bending stuff can even deliver us a point, which is maybe the point.

The Moth: A Fable

S OMETIMES IT CAN SEEM like your mind is a moth in re-
verse, barreling toward lamps unlit.

Yet, sometimes it's just the opposite, and, if you remember it, perhaps you can rest everything in the cradle
of this moment.

You are nine years old in blue shirtsleeves sitting in
the school gym. Your brother, a seventh grader, is on
stage. The play is called *The Dames of Dragonfly Ditch*.
And his character's name is Fairlane. Fairlane sits in a
kitchen talking to a girl who is terribly in love with him.
He tells her he has come for sugar. They talk. Finally he
leaves. After a few moments, he returns. "I forgot something," he says. The girl pipes up brightly, "Fairlane, you
forgot to kiss me goodbye?" And your brother says,
"No! I forgot the sugar!"

Everyone erupts! The kids all laugh so hard! It is so
surprising! So perfect! He's left. He comes back. She

thinks it is to kiss her. And he says, "No, I forgot the sugar!" Just like that. The sugar! He doesn't want to kiss her. He wants the sugar! He shocks her. He shocks everyone. You never forget that line. No funny thing you ever heard would be more hilarious than that.

That laughter might have set up a wall of protection around you, if you wanted it to, from anything foul or seamy in the world. A laughter that bore into you some kind of love (?) not necessarily for your brother but for the idea of brother. He as an actor and his perfect timing, crushing the flighty hopeful female lead with his sharp asexual young feller voice, "No, I forgot the sugar!" A thing high up on a stage whose name was not Brother but Defender. Defender from any swooning female or things far worse. Far more practical than any distant incarnation.

God Is Gød

J UST WHEN YOU THINK you have this God, you don't. It is all about God, but it is all about you. The problem of free will. Always the problem of free and liberated will. Every decision in your adult life, says God, is yours to make. But even though it is all in your hands, don't put pressure on yourself! Take off the pressure of all your wrenching choices and give them all to God—hand them over to Christ! It is all on you to give it all to Christ because it is all on Christ.

And yet, Christ has no body but your body, says Teresa of Avila. He has no hands, no feet on earth but yours. Yours are the eyes with which God bestows compassion on the world. You have free will to turn your life over to God, who then is in charge and who then empowers you so that you are in charge and Christ is Lord.

(And the Lord in the Los Angeles cathedral not only hangs from a cross but his skin is rippled waves, as one burned up, a corpse pulled from a raging fire.)

Jean-Luc Marion gives God a new name. He uses a "St. Andrew's" cross to cross out the metaphysical meaning of the name "God." "To cross out God," says Marion, in fact, indicates and recalls that God crosses out our thought because he saturates it." We quit the old title "God" because even using the name can make us think we've got him in our sights and under control. Naming God as if God is a thing we can name—how brash. It is like the assertion of Meister Eckhart that there is a God beyond God; or the Fourth Lateran Council that claims whatever we can positively say about God is outdone in spades by what we cannot say about God.

Marion says God's mystery is so overwhelming that it destroys our thought of God. It does this destroying not from a distance but from close range. God's mystery saturates us and drowns our thought. His presence overwhelms our thinking. It overwhelms every created thing. There is no distance, no place we go that this God does not want to go, or already is. Marion says it is this saturated sense of divine presence that helps us to "bypass thinking." God bypasses the abyss of our fear and powerlessness.

This saturation puts to rout any need for us to think about God. Saying "Gød"—a new word that is not even a word, because God can never be bound by a single word—gets us closer to simple, direct, mystical awareness of God's presence. Remove the word, take away the neatly placed letters and just, I don't know, exist. God as simply *what is around*. There is no reaching for it. God is revealed to us. We don't make it happen. We just accept.

But still, we don't see him face-to-face! This "apophatic" approach—this "no-to-yes" to understanding God—acknowledges we cannot plainly name God and how God does what he does. We can only gesture to him, like scarecrows in a windstorm. As the philosopher Jozef Fekete claims, we can only "stammer out a speechless breath of understanding." We cannot see or comprehend this thing called the Divine, but we know it is there because the straw man is spinning around. Must be quite a thing out there! Look at that baby whirl!

God is part and parcel of Jesus, a man with a torso, four limbs, thirty-two teeth in his mouth—all so clear, so obvious, what more do we need? We know everything we have to know about God through Jesus. The Savior is straightforward and clear: his actions are decisive; he gives commands; he tells riveting tales.

Nevertheless, even the words of this fleshly historical man are, at times, baffling. His words and actions are mysterious and, for centuries, arguments have been made and sermons delivered and books written debating what he meant and how to live what he meant. The Prince of Peace tells us that he will bring a sword, that we should hate our parents, and that we can pick up serpents like ropes of licorice. Clarity? Is clarity about the things of

God the grandest illusion of them all? Is it a grail that never existed in the first place?

The *Catechism of the Catholic Church*, a text mostly rife with clarity, is a wonderful thing. It makes you think someone's got this all figured out. "If a man commits evil, the just judgment of conscience can remain within him as the witness to the universal truth of the good, at the same time as the evil of his particular choice" (*CCC*, Part 3, Article 6, No. 1781). Who doesn't need that kind of precision? A feeling that someone on this earth has risen above, has achieved the mountaintop view. An intelligent soul has laid out the grid, turned the wilderness into a city. Someone has made hay of all this mess.

Or consider the Dogmatic Constitution on the Church, *Lumen Gentium*, "Light of the Nations." (So assertive, so confident!) It is all in here! How everything happened and why! The church, human salvation, the mystical presence of God. Life has a constitution. A charter to assure us that things are on the right track. "At the end of time [the Church] will achieve her glorious fulfillment. Then, as may be read in the holy Fathers, all just men from the time of Adam, 'from Abel, the just one, to the last of the elect,' will be gathered together with the Father in the universal church."

It is right there. It's going to happen. Put it in the bank. The church will reconcile all unto itself. So clear, so convincing—words that barely need to be said because it's so evident!

St. Ignatius of Loyola, the founder of the Jesuits, nails the meaning of everything in one sentence: "Human beings are created to praise reverence and serve the divine majesty and by means of this to save their souls."

And we had to look so hard for the purpose of life? It was right here all along.

Or take Fr. Jose Maniyangat. According to a flyer advertising a healing retreat in Portland, Oregon, this priest "was taken by his guardian angel to visit heaven, hell, and purgatory in a death experience from a traffic accident in 1985 and came back to life to continue his ministry." This is starting to sound very promising. "When Maniyangat appeared before the Lord, Jesus told him: I want you to go back to the world. In your second life you will be an instrument of peace and healing to my people. . . . Everything is possible for you with my grace."

There's your man. Invite Fr. Maniyangat into your home and make him tell all. He's been there. He knows from experience. Kidnap this cleric and don't let him go, so he'll be with you whenever something horrible comes up and you can exquisitely hear him say: *Please.* (Dismissive wave of the hand.) *I've been there. You've got nothing to worry about.*

Or at least wear drops of Father Jose's sweat in a locket around your neck and let his knowledge and power hustle you through any pain and madness that comes your way. *We got this one*, whispers the priest around your neck as the beams start falling. *God is knowable. We had a very nice conversation. He gave explicit instruction. Listen up.*

Nevertheless, most of the time, we look through a cracked glass, sight through a thick window in a jail, the reflection off a camouflage shirt. We look for glints of the divine and we recognize we will never get the full show. The burned body of Jesus is not here. Where have they taken him? Is this okay, that he is out of sight, the thirty-three-year-old Nazorean, the ageless God—that he is nowhere to be found?

(But he crackles alive in the Eucharist . . . and a host is a very small round thing that does not speak.)

Christians have given their lives to someone who is not there. They have founded their lives on a ghost . . . on a story . . . on a series of rituals handed down. The life of a vowed religious is a grand wager that these stories will do. That prayer alone is as consoling as marriage. Not to idealize marriage, or any old-timey shacking up. Jesuits have community, companions, friendship, and this is stirring and real.

Still. You are twined up with a kneeler, a prayer bench, a cardboard box in a corner. A nervy bet that this is okay. That living for the unseen and the untouchable can actually be nice. We are "in relationship," all people are, with something we cannot directly see or touch or hear, and isn't it fair to ask if this is not even a bit disturbing? We don't see the wizard behind the screen.

Oh, maybe there is relief in that. For if we did see him, if we were all Fr. Jose Maniyangat, wouldn't we all feel more pressure? But you saw Christ. You heard him speak those words. Why are you still the way you are?

"Do not grieve or complain that you were born in a time when you can no longer see God in the flesh," says Augustine. "He did not in fact take this privilege from you. As he says, 'Whatever you have done to the least of my brothers, you did to me.'"

Yes, Christ is in the least. Serve them and you are serving him. We take care of the poor—no matter how distressingly human they are—and as it says in the gospel, we become sheep, the kingdom prepared for us. The goats, who did not serve Christ sick, naked, or jailed, they will go down. We sheep will go up. We have been taught to see a glowing messiah in every afflicted soul out there.

For Marion, this revelation—the *who and what of God*—is . . . love. Boring, non-philosophical love.

"To think Gød, therefore, outside of ontological difference," Marion says, "outside the question of Being, as well, risks the unthinkable, indispensable, but impassable." In other words, while God is always beyond any sense of what a human tongue can put form to, what fits all those categories—unthinkable, indispensable, impassable—is what St. John proposes: "God is love."

Ah, the old conversation-ender: God is love! God is good and God is love! All of that theo-philosophical talk finally gets down to the old chestnut "God is love." Why didn't you say so in the first place? Everything now makes sense. Armed with this certainty, all those lottery balls click in all the right spots for everyone's ticket, and the goats too end up at the good place because God is love. And according to Paul, love never fails. Love. Never. Fails.

After all, isn't that your experience? Love has never failed you, isn't that right?

The Wheels on the Car Go Round and Round

T HE WRECKS, the Midwestern car wrecks, and the memorial posters on empty lockers, graduation pictures looming over a casket. My God. Brandon graduates, a year later gets killed in a car accident, and you wonder: What happens to the family when every kid in the school hugs them coming out of the memorial service? The Lakota handshake, the Lakota hug. Do they heal? Do they go numb?

And what happens when the family wraps up in a star quilt the girl who drove the car? What is passed in the blood when this happens? What is borne in a hurricane of harsh and deadly love that could hit you right then? What terrible madness comes upon us all?

You go over to the family's house the night it happens. The photographs are out, and the mother talks about how he used to do push-ups, used to call home all the time. He suddenly becomes the best kid; the Best Kid! How did he become the Best Kid? Did we always know it? That he was the best? Or did it emerge from some burrow, did it just come out once he was gone? O Brandon! Senior Prom King! Theater kid. The vampire in the film *Toma* made on the school grounds.

Is this what we garnered here on the night he died, the kid who was not shy of saying "How are you?" to the teachers and the parents? The kid who in college called his mom all the time. Who did push-ups! Who knew this skinny kid did push-ups? In his striped knit shirts, push-ups! I'm getting stronger mom!

Maybe he died so, indeed, we would suddenly know what a great guy he was. Maybe his death flushed out of the sagebrush of Pine Ridge his goodness. His loveliness was released into the air, a conifer whose seeds don't come out until the heat of a great fire. (This is not true—everyone knew Brandon was a wonderful young man.)

But any death flushes love out of our systems. We did not know how much we loved, what capacity we had.

A man in scrubs sees his child burst through the seawall. I never knew I could love someone so instantly and so completely. The birth of a child flushes out a splendor of love and the death of a child like Brandon flushes out a rage of love. The joy and the torment of it all bound up in one cinema vampire moving slowly through the snow among the scrubby hills behind the high school.

And Carrie two years later. I taught her "Catholic Rites" and "Faith and Justice." She graduated, I moved on, and then a car crash. She went through her own rites, was given her own rank injustice. Carrie, with the purple-streaked hair. Carrie, lugging the wrestling scorebook around or painting theater sets. Carrie, who as a sophomore pleasantly denies the existence of God and as a senior believes, praying unashamedly in front of the class.

I spoke on the phone with Carrie's mother, who said that on the fourth day there was an *inipi*, a sweat, and the medicine man told everyone that Carrie's spirit had visited all the places she had ever wanted to go to in the world. Carrie was happy and now was ready to make her journey to the spirit world.

That week, I also spoke with her classmate Shaina as she was driving out to begin freshman year at a very cool college. She was so sad for Carrie but excited for her own future. Both of these things, the way they were together—a far-off university and a young spirit's ascent, a mournful sweat lodge and a tiny dorm fridge, a powdered face in a coffin, a girl studying fiercely in a blond wood carrel: they were, in their own way, the colors of fancy dance regalia, whirling around and flashing together, the dark and the light, the electric green and the brown, the yellow, red, and black and it is all together. We deserve everything, we deserve nothing; the world is made for us, the world is not made for us, not one bit of it.

And the crashes where I'm from. I can see them from a thousand miles away, imagine them in my neighborhood. Omaha, three gentle vowels and a soft h. No hint of what unpleasant things can happen there. The Gilroy boy, a junior, dies in a car wreck and Mrs. Thompson's son dies of a heart attack that causes a car crash or dies in the crash that follows the heart attack, and two guys going fishing on graduation night get killed on the road and the Tells' daughter dies in a car wreck and her sister is badly injured, O stop reading, stop! And the Lakes' little daughter dies not in a car wreck but at home, a child at play and then she is gone. The small Lake girl dies and then yes, a car wreck years later, their son at age eighteen. How do the parents do it? What do they hold on to?

The family buries them both but they don't bury, of course, God, because they need God. God has "passively" cast these kids down so their parents will cling to God all the more.

(And these aren't the world's dispossessed, to be sure, those veins of humanity where untimely death is a given. These are suburban people of the American Midwest with all the privileges of their class and hue. These deaths come along and pockmark the gray streets of, pretty much, Caucasians! Shall even we white people suffer? We all know the dark forces of this world have their weapons trained with great precision, so to speak, on the brown and black and all those on the margins. But Lord, you really mean business, don't you? You even go after the colonizers.)

God "allows" these tragedies, and either you flee God altogether or you decide you need him all the more. God is both supply and demand, labor and management, healer and destroyer, scarcity and surplus. God siphons away whatever credit you have accrued so you have to come begging back to him for your daily cut. We, the battered partners, we keep coming back.

The Lord went after the daughter who once showed up at our soccer game to watch her younger brother. She was a high school senior of the type you can't fully believe exists in your modest city, all that woolen Gap-ish beauty, perhaps a gray rolled-neck sweater, maybe hands balled up beneath the sleeves in the damp spring, buttercream blonde hair whose perfect natural condition is Misted Upon. Misted upon while she is shivering serenely on the sidelines of parochial school soccer matches. And then a few short years pass, not too many, and this girl....

O these wrecks. I have so little to offer, just terrible stories, it would seem. All we want is a lodestar.

SUFFERING GIVES YOU the power to make rooms go hush when you enter. It starts you on a habit of running marathons, or becoming wildly more productive at work, sealing off with a whirlwind of activity the memory of your shuddering loss and making maybe a lot of money and then giving most of it away, starting a foundation named after the one you lost. Suffering incites you as a member of Congress to pass bills to combat the disease your wife died from even though you have been for decades the kind of congressman who, perhaps, never passed a bill to help anyone's needless suffering. Sometimes, uninvited suffering is a relief. It helps you get your mind off other things.

Sleep

THREE DAYS WITHOUT PRAYER, and God does not exist anymore. How does God vanish so easily? How does his felt mercy up and disappear? Just because we are not disciplined enough to sit and be quiet and contemplate the loving eternal emptiness? Why can't God lie like a cool cloth on the forehead, something felt and comforting every moment? A Jesuit priest once said that most spiritual desolation is fatigue. Sleep. We all just need sleep.

Or is spiritual desolation just forgetting? If only we remembered to read the Bible. If only we prayed more. Maybe being with God and charmed by mere existence and trusting things will be okay is a simple matter of discipline. Getting up early, praying, working out, and eating right. It's all in your hands. It is all about you. God is just there. Getting close to God, finding serenity in a harsh world, it just takes discipline! Stay with it! To the kids in jail—join a basketball league and get to church and stay off the streets. That will solve everything! You can do it! When it gets hard, just stick with it!

Mary Magdalene and the worst moment of her life—not only did they torture and kill her friend and savior, but now they have stolen his body. All she wants to know is where they have taken him. Can you please tell me, sir? For the love of God, couldn't they leave well enough alone? After all they did to him, and it still wasn't enough?

And then she turns. She turns, and there, in front of her.

Stay one minute longer, and the Lord will appear.

The Tibetan monk Thich Nhat Hanh instructs us to simply smile. Raise those muscles up, he says, and you will be infinitely more peaceful and joyful. You will be like Thich Nhat Hanh. He is celibate, he smiles, he is happy! It's all on you!

The Dark Horse

W HEN THE PLANES took down the towers and sent the smudged leaflets into the subways and launched two wars, they also did something less devastating but still, in its own way, impacting. They knocked out the gigantic television antenna that rested on top of One World Trade Center, the North Tower. So that if you lived in the city and did not have a cable hookup, the only station you could watch was WWOR. And WWOR did not show Yankees games.

This meant that when New York made it to the seventh game of the World Series that year, people who had only regular TV could not watch the game at home. Where I was on that night had only regular TV, so we listened to it on the radio.

I was a year out from joining the Jesuits, acting, writing, serving café con leches. That night, I was at the apartment of a candidate for the New York City Council,

Kwong Hui. Kwong was a skinny, thirty-ish organizer, who managed to be a tad humorless and fairly engaging at the same time. He had made noise in New York labor circles for, among other things, taking part in efforts that exposed the maltreatment of sweatshop workers in Chinatown. Results included winning back pay for garment workers employed by contractors for Kathy Lee Gifford's clothing line, amping up his profile all the more.

Kwong took this momentum and ran for elected office during an opportune year, when term limits were ending the careers of many long-time city council members.

And then New York's Election Day came, and so did the planes. The election was quickly canceled that morning. Kwong and his core volunteers regrouped and turned the campaign into a relief effort for people, primarily in public housing in Chinatown and the Lower East Side of Manhattan, his would-be constituency.

In the city, the terrible flyers, the gray and black dust, the acid shock, the posters and messages of peace scrawled all over a George Washington statue in Union Square. For weeks, the air downtown was sulfurous. Later, a man who had been a medic in Vietnam wrote that the smell was, in part, the odor of dead, rotting bodies.

In Kwong's district, they were staggering from their businesses being shut down, their phones not working, and the mental and emotional devastation. We knocked on doors, checked on elders, agitated to get air purifiers from FEMA.

I followed the Yankees with half an eye—catching TV highlights through restaurant windows, a headline in a newsstand. They were making a somewhat improbable run for another World Series title. Games were close, playoff leads reeled back and forth. Their young short-stop, Derek Jeter, was doing extraordinary things on de-fense to keep the Yankees alive. Each time New York won a big game, Joe Torre would bring onto the field everyone's hero, Rudy Giuliani. The Yankees fought their way past the Oakland A's, then the Seattle Mariners, and finally into the Series.

In the meantime, the election had been rescheduled and our relief work turned back into a campaign. When the World Series went to a seventh game, it took place on Sunday night, November 4, two days before the election.

We were sorting flyers and posters and listening to the game on the radio and it was tied. Who knew where this was going? But then, in the top of the eighth inning, the young center fielder, Alfonso Soriano, hit a solo home run and the Yankees took a one-run lead.

The Yankees were suddenly winning late in game seven of the World Series two months after the city had been attacked by terrorists in planes. Two months after the devastation, the grief beyond what a surviving body seemed capable of bearing, the pain sent forth in waves over the entire region, those firemen sitting helplessly in front of their open red garages surrounded by flowers and candles and cards from school kids, the economy sunk, the air toxic, and the lesser evil of the just war that followed the bombing, and wondering how much traction evil loses when it is simply "lesser," and Talia, the organizer from Queens with whom you have fallen into a half-hearted relationship, and we could go on about those days, couldn't we, pages, books, theories, heroics, lights, shadows, and shadows of shadows....

Nevertheless, coming on to end this madness for at least one night—to heal it for the space of a few champagne-soaked moments—was the best pitcher in the known universe.

This pitcher, Mariano Rivera, was going to get them out, the other team, because that is what he always did. The Yankees were going to win. Even though it would feel to some unjust because it would be their fourth title in a row and they were rich and they were the Yankees, none of that really mattered. It didn't matter because this moment was right, and lifted, and it was all going to work out.

Listening to a tight, high-stakes sports event on the radio, seeing nothing, you exist in dark territory. It is as if you have to trust the team even more. Give yourself over to these unseen men trying to deliver, in this case, whatever victory a reeling city can lay its hands on. With no images to follow, you are almost closer to them in the dark than you would be in the light.

Add to this the sorrow still hanging over the ashy streets outside, and the odds against an under-funded dark horse candidate trying to change the world one city council seat at a time, and Talia's caramel skin and faint charming lisp that, still, one cannot live by. All of this somehow etches the sounds coming over the airwaves much more deeply into your heart. The towers go down, and the antenna, and so much else, and a few weeks later, we are thrown blind and helpless into the hands of this stacked, overpaid, unflustered, gutty, endearing ball club.

And it is the bottom of the ninth, and Rivera walks to the mound.

And then things fall apart.

We don't need to fully document it here. Quickly: there is a hit. And there is another hit, this one back to the mound. And Rivera throws the ball into center field, and the runners are safe and things go on like this and suddenly the Diamondbacks have won the World Series and the Yankees have not.

We turned off the radio. We finished folding the brochures. Everyone went home. I left with Talia. The Yankees had lost and the towers smoldered, and two days later, Kwong Hui the sweatshop crusader would lose, and lose bad.

While everyone soldiered on after 9-11, and our little group had done positive things for lower Manhattan, and it was *just a baseball game*, still. It all seemed to point to something more insidious out there. Nothing good ever really takes hold. We are all compromised. Violence is a gene no religion can excise. Sin is bigger than everything that is. You can try, but you won't get there, wherever it is you really want to go. *This team deserved to win.* September 11 should have just been an election day. This city ought to have been left alone. But it was not left alone. The city had visitors. We are made like seeds in a crisp pod for these tragic ends. Who knows what we deserve?

So much love at birth and even more at death. The heart expanded in a delivery room ready to take on all enemies, or contracted at a funeral so small and tight because it does not want ever to feel that kind of pain again. Julie died in the previous worst thing on American soil and we traveled from points all over to Oklahoma for the funeral. There we met her father, Bud, who quickly became a street fighter against the kind of talk radio that incited the Timothy McVeighs of the world.

She always looked kind of sleepy, Julie Welch did, or a little high, even if she wasn't, and just interesting in her modified cat's-eye glasses, red hair, whisper of a bouffant, coming upon you in the dorm hallway and gazing with head-tilting concern, *How are you?* She would listen to growling female rock bands you surely are not familiar with; strolling everywhere serenely; becoming more religious as college went on, but not in a way that made her, like, mean.

After college she went home and translated for Spanish speakers in the Social Security office. And then Tim McVeigh parked a truck.

And the father's bitterness and rage and McVeigh up for the death penalty. And Bud remembering the day he was driving with Julie and the radio announcer starts talking about capital punishment. *Dad, do you believe in the death penalty? I don't think I do.*

I don't think I do. And everything changes. The father is done with it. No more violence. Bud tells me all this on my pilgrimage after I hitchhike from New Mexico and visit him in Oklahoma seven years after the bombing. He reaches out to Timothy McVeigh's father and sets up a meeting. Realizes this man is going to lose his kid like Bud lost his daughter. They come together, two fathers grieving. Bud fights against the death penalty. He fights to save the life of the man who killed his kid.

And after Timothy McVeigh is executed anyway, Bud goes on to agitate against the death penalty wholesale with Sister Helen Prejean.

At Julie's funeral, her boyfriend, who is in the Air Force, recites a poem he wrote for her, based on her name, Julie. J is for joyous. U is for... I don't remember what U is for. Understanding? They had talked of engagement. Her college girlfriends seethe in the pews. This is not Julie. It's pathetic. This guy was trying to convince her to marry him and make her into a proper Air Force–wife Christian? Really? This is not her. Dating the type of upright guy who would, with a true believer's memorial service *it's-all-God's-plan* smile, make a poem with the letters of her name. Ridiculous.

(Or maybe he just really loved her and smiled because he didn't know what else to do.)

Julie who had the longing in her voice, a voice that was quite possibly more cheerful if there actually was something wrong in your life, and the sleepy eyes and the mustard sweater and vaguely Oklahoma hair. Julie who faked my ID and badly. Who was responsible? Who made this happen? Why did God let Julie become a dead girl whose most memorable eulogy was an acrostic?

DEATH IS AN ENGINE that hums through a house giving it clarity and purpose.

Aqedah

CONSIDER, DEAR FRIENDS, the Aqedah. A bible passage with a title, momentous. Aqedah. Like Nativity, Transfiguration, Annunciation. Like Holocaust, Waterboarding, Jihad, Firebomb. Aqedah. Maybe we ought to just write it out, the Aqedah, the whole passage, and then go about our business. Because it probably needs little commentary, it can just stand alone with no further explanation. Because this story is the be-all and end-all of pure biblical insanity.

> "Take your son, Isaac, your only one, whom you love." . . . "Stay here with the donkey, while the boy and I go on over there." . . . So Abraham took the wood for the burnt offering. . . . "Here are the fire and the wood, but where is the sheep for the burnt offering?" . . . Then Abraham reached out and took the knife. . . .

Need we say more? Why are the pews empty, these days? Given stories like this, why has any pew ever been filled?

Three days, Abraham, you walked silently to your awful mission. All we can see is your terrible silence. The author shows what you did; he does not tell how you felt about it. The finest example of "show not tell" perhaps in all of literature. We are told absolutely nothing of what was going through your mind as you walked to the execution of your son. We can only imagine. The Aqedah is just dialogue and action, and all the more chilling for it. Abraham walks. What does he feel? What kind of man just up and does this, as if he was asked to go fetch a pile of river stones?

Take your son, your only one, whom you love. The author, as they say, raises the stakes. God reminds Abraham how this will be for him—how difficult it will be for him who complained to God that he had no offspring and so was promised by God not only a child but descendants as numerous as the stars. God reminding the old man that this is unpleasant business, being invited to audition for the role of Great Obeyer where the primary question is: Can you plunge a knife into your kid? Your son, your only one, whom you love . . . ?

Perhaps the madness of this pericope can be handled by my decisive grad school paper on the topic:

The story's *Sitz im Leben*, according to Van Seters, comes from an Iphigenia motif, where the "gods demand the sacrifice of a beloved child and then at the last moment an animal is substituted, miraculously" (Van Seters, 129). Iphigenia was a daughter of Agamemnon who was nearly sacrificed to Artemis but saved by Artemis and later made a priestess.

It is just a myth, people. It is a way of understanding things. It is a story like other stories. Let's take down the temperature a bit. Van Seters has made this all right. The *Sitz im Leben* tells us all we need to know. It reassures us by placing the story in the stream of so many other wild and disturbing stories out there, and now we can go about our business. These stories happen, the near sacrificing of offspring. They are a usual convention in literature. We can rise above and see this from a more reasonable plane. Okay?

Yet, a Greek myth is different. An ancient Greek tale is something taken apart stone by stone in an intense undergrad classroom, or pored over in some sixteen-year-old's moody bedroom. It has academic heft, it gets in the bloodstream in a different way. The very place where it is confronted—college seminars or a shadowy teen cave—can serve to declaw it, make it appropriately distanced. The Iphigenia motif is not read in a religious ceremony upon which hinges, as it is said, the redemption of the world.

But this story—the "Sacrifice of Isaac," "The Testing of Abraham," "The Testing of All Sane Believers"—it's something we read in church! In church with carpet and candles and hymnals and rouge high on the cheekbones. This story of the slow and deliberate murder of a child, engineered by the same God who commands us to love our neighbor as ourself: it is read in respectable company. This monstrous thing is proclaimed in a room full of small children! We throw this bloody carcass into the middle of the baptismal font and cry to the congregation: *Well, what do you have to say now?*

It is a miracle that the sheetrock doesn't collapse, the bulletin doesn't spontaneously combust, the cruets don't shatter whenever this story is read.

But still, there is hope! There is always, with God, hope! My paper goes on:

> The story was possibly an etiological cult legend of a sanctuary that hosted the sacrifice of humans. And so the legend was intended to show how human sacrifice came to be rejected.

We can all breathe a sigh of relief. God really is good! The story of a father sacrificing his only son, the one he loves, is a lesson for *doing just the opposite*. God wanted us to learn something and used a bit of a shock getting there, but boy we get it now, don't we? Thought you had me, Lord, but you were just showing us what not to do! It is all about not killing your kid.

My professor read this interpretation—this view of "The Testing" as a lesson for rejecting child sacrifice—

and kindly wrote in red ink: "I doubt that. Nothing suggests it in the story."

And, when I detailed for him how other scholars had also endorsed the story as a rejection of child sacrifice, this teacher wrote: "I would not get enticed by these kinds of efforts to rob the text of its meaning."

Do not be lured into those sturdy "explainings away" of this horrible story, that oh so quickly usher us past its very dark edge. Do not placidly reject the literal meaning of this text. Tarry, young scholar, lest you immediately scurry off to a comforting place: *There is a clear and simple historically grounded answer to this. It was actually there to do the opposite of what we think. It's just a life lesson.*

No, stay with this. Let it work you over. Consider the God who would do this. Imagine how you would respond. (What child are you being asked to sacrifice?) What do you really want to do with this? Don't swipe from this text its ability to destroy your notions of who God is and how God operates, a love that comes in the form of a birdbath, a flying fish, a fantastic pair of puddle stompers. Maybe it's not really like that.

And when I further wrote in my paper that the story was about Abraham "trusting" God, my teacher, Dr. DiStefano, wrote: "Is it??? Did Abraham 'trust'? Or did he simply 'obey'? I mean, what leads you to think 'it would all turn out O.K.'?"

Trust is more spiritual. It sounds warmer. You trust and you have a sense it is going somewhere. Obeying, however, feels more...religious. Dogmatic. Doing a thing because you are commanded to obey, because if it is a thing that you are commanded to obey, it is the type of thing that should be obeyed. Otherwise, why the necessity to command that it be obeyed? The circular reasoning of sheer certainty.

And thus and so, apparently, "The Testing of Abraham" is a story about the need to obey God. To obey God at all costs. And what a thing it is to obey that one! For what is the reward? Doesn't God command (or "allow") these tragedies and still demand our obedience? God doesn't whisk away your vampire son, Brandon, from the realm of the undead, and then say, "Well I've put you through a lot, haven't I? You deserve time off from my commands and precepts. You don't have to obey me. You don't have to do my bidding."

No, God lets your kid die, your city collapse, and then still demands your allegiance. God made Abraham go through the worst thing—three days to think about it!—and then declared: "Great, you did it! Now having proven to you I am just about the cruelest teacher that ever existed, I grant you the opportunity to be my student eternally!"

Tevye's classic line in *Fiddler on the Roof* is a wry Yiddish complaint, played for a laugh: "I know, I know. We are Your chosen people. But once in a while can't You choose someone else?"

But, oh, is there a dark current beneath those words? We are chosen to the brink of death, and that journey—

its waves and tremors—must lodge in the soul. Which bears the larger footprint: the intervention by the angel and its sheer weeping relief? Or the fact that you were called to do something so unthinkable that it needed intervening at all?

JOHN OF THE CROSS shines a thin beam of hope into all our darkness, a glow of sense within our bewilderment at God. "[Souls in the dark night]," he writes, "are nearer to him when they are least aware of it . . . when you are near him the infirmity of your vision makes the darkness denser."

We can't see things well when they are too near to us, when we are saturated by their presence. We are used to seeing love at a distance—love in dreams as opposed to love in reality. But when it really and truly enters your life, love upends your soul. In what seems to be our worst times, John is saying, God is with us even more closely.

In other words, everything you thought was love—romance, precious feelings, dazzling gifts—gets shattered when you experience someone who truly loves you. A stray and chancy boyfriend, adorable selector of mediocre wines and shabby motels, his presence, no matter how inconsistent, is sheer euphoria. But can anyone live off euphoria?

Over time, though, he transforms into something called a man. One whose love is so authentic he will sacrifice his wealth, home, future, everything for you.

This love is so unbelievable you don't even recognize it. You are used to sad next mornings. But this love calls you out and you don't always know where it is calling you to. Seeing the pure love of God—as opposed to how you previously saw it—is astonishing. It can take the soul by storm. Real love is frightening.

In the dark night, the soul that has made some progress on the journey toward God and has grown to love the feelings of consolation it has attained in its spiritual life now goes through a period where those "attachments" are withdrawn. And one must seek more purely God himself, not the things that speak of God or seem to be God.

John says that the dark night of the soul begins "when God, gradually drawing them out of the state of beginners (those who practice meditation on the spiritual road) begins to place them in the state of proficients (those who are already contemplatives) so that by passing through this state they might reach that of the perfect, which is the divine union with God."

The darkness can be very difficult, but as Elaine Yaryan writes: "According to John the darkness is not evil at all. He believed that during the dark night of the soul God is invading the human soul with his pure light. When the light shines up all the frailties and hidden evil of the heart it appears to the soul that she is estranged from God, that she has been cut off from him."

Ruth Burrows describes the dark night as a purging. "In between the bouts of violent cleanings, the patient knows periods of delightful well-being and imagines he is fully healed, only to be submerged again in another intense purgation." It is terrifying to lose the old comforting poisons that got us this far. "The purgation continues until everything that is alien to God is destroyed."

For some people, however, "violent cleanings" can be devastating. Writes Burrows: "Those emotionally insecure, with a low self-image, for instance, are going to find all this much harder to bear than the secure person with a proper sense of personal value...we must at the same time be ready to acknowledge that there may well be a truly mystical experience underneath a lot of neurotic symptoms."

This discussion of the soul's progress through spiritual trials, no matter how mystical they are, begets the same question; the lawyer's redirection: Is God inflicting evil into our lives, a privation, a lack of the felt good? Is God deliberately making this night happen? Because it can seem like the old adage, "God doesn't give you any more than you can handle," is a finely wrought lie. A man once told me that growing up, he and his sister were often just left to go on their own. "And you could just tell," he said. "We were the type of kids you could do anything to." And adults did do things to these children. They did things.

And things done to children crash down through the generations, sometimes doubled down, tripled, and brutally. Through all this long dark night, some will be led closer to God, and some will be led deeply into nowhere.

A Snake, Quiet and Still: A Fable

I T IS A FACT, dear friends, that coming upon any large snake unmoving in short weeds anywhere changes forever the ground where it rests. It utterly changes your life, too, no? The snake on the country school grounds, glimmering, still, its colors you try to guess at, a color to fear, a color to walk by carefully, like you would a reeling gabbling man wielding a dark pipe on a dark street. The snake in the gravel path you spy one morning has then suddenly marked it forever—you will not go by this place for as long as you live without imagining it there again, without the slight shudder that, over time, eventually takes place only in the depths of you so that you do not feel it, but still the shudder is there.

The snake in your path at the country school, the snake holding its own, the snake that has made an encampment, like the Poor People's Campaign, in D.C. in '68, where, after King was shot, cops destroyed their shacks—or was that the Bonus Army, the World War I veteran protesters who gathered on the lawn of the U.S. Capitol that the Army itself broke up, or was it both?

This snake, like an avenging army encamped somewhat close to the school, a place where you're trying to do good things. The snake sits comfortably, silently, and your heart awakens—you remember you have a heart, it beats and you hear it...and the funeral of your little brother, and afterwards your girlfriend putting her arm around you in the car and you were wanting to smack her: *what will this arm do for me* and then hating yourself and hating the black molding of the dashboard, the smooth engine, all the perfectly working parts, as if they mock or pretend to live in a universe in which everything works perfectly. The serpent enters your home, your mind. This is the South; you've never been here before.

The snake goes to bed with you, has crawled into your blood and rests with you, and you will never look at that patch of ground again and think a thought unclouded by the awareness, for at least an instant, that there was a snake here. Something that you knew existed, had seen before, snakes, but until then didn't know really existed. Danger and sin come down from the hills.

The snake has no answer. The snake sits there, knowing nothing. The snake gives you nothing, it keeps its secrets. Who art thou, teacher? Thou teachest these children, but I shall take away whatever thou givest them. Even if I never strike, just knowing I am here will tamp their aspirations back into the ground, make buried treasures of these kids, all their glorious potential sunk beneath the dirt.

Who wants to leave this school when there are so many serpents around? We ring the grounds, we've got everything covered.

The snake reminds you that things won't always be so easy, but hey, you can always walk away from it. Is it really so fearful to be around a snake you spy from a good distance in daylight? With plenty of space to turn around and go elsewhere? The snake lets you feel your own power. The snake shines into your face: choice. You are a person and have a choice: you dominate this snake, you are the master of it.

A few short months ago your little brother drowned and you rolled the windows up and took your hand away from hers and things went on like this, and in three weeks she was done with you and you traveled across the country down to the place you thought would be an appropriate dumping ground for your indissoluble grief—a poor town in a poor state with a people who are historically, constitutionally, professionals at grieving. Your grief would mingle in the vat of the greater cultural and social grief of Mississippi and would be seasoned, and translated into something new, and you would teach math. Your grief would become useful, turn tragedy into a spade to dig some kids out of their ignorance.

What of the snake? What did it want from us? How were we to respond? With catcalls and fey glances? Would the snake turn us into gritty New York debutantes? The snake was wheedling its way into our hearts. The snake was like war, in modern times, with all we know and can know, and the ways we can talk to each other: the laying of the transatlantic cable, for crying out loud, and we still have wars? Thus it is with snakes. They are still out there and it's rather shocking. They are in our daughter's playthings, waiting—these serpents. There by the dump it sits, out where the air still smells of poll tax, where, against all county ordinances, the school burns the trash every Friday and the smell spreads over the whole compound, a faint whiff of a pleasant summer marshmallow roasting, but then a turn, a turn into something malevolent, a turn, and so the snake takes its stand by the garbage dump and both of them, snake and fire pit, radiate out to the wider community that things are not as wonderful as you thought they were. As you thought you were healing, the kids were being healed. Your sorrow was being turned to good. But then, four of the best students at your all-black school get kicked out for jumping a white kid and weren't the races supposed to be reversed in terms of who was attacking whom, which was why you were here? But facts are facts.

Snake, primal evil, embodied wickedness (*it's just not okay that snakes still exist*) and there you are, crushed, your brother just playing by the dock and carried out, just taken out and that was the end of it. You were away, it wasn't your fault, the body in the casket like a three-headed cow, or smashed-up tabernacle, or some other wrong thing. The peasantry bowing their heads as the king goes by. Eleanor never really understood how Franklin did it until the train moved slowly from Warm Springs to Washington, with all the people lined along the tracks, weeping and silent, and then she understood how much they loved him. The heart blasted at birth and death. How much of Jesus can we bear?

Your little brother, his death like citrus that cuts through the oil of anointing, the triviality, or whatever you thought life was about. Why didn't he try out for varsity? And you thinking that somehow it was your responsibility to make sure another human lived his life as you needed him to, and only when the citrus soaked in and he was gone did you see vividly how much he meant to you; how he was sewn into your chest like a monogram, worn around your neck like a scapular, and how varsity faded into the dust of the dust that makes up dust.

The snake keeps watch over your thoughts. Maybe it is not a thing of evil. Maybe it is just an animal that startles you in its path. Maybe nothing means anything. The coiling, hissing thing is so ancient and eternal and turns its way through all questions you take up here, it just is. You have no idea. Maybe it is, obviously, oh so clearly the devil, and maybe it is just...

The Pigs of Kohima

IN A SMALL WOODEN PEN on a hillside near Shillong, in the state of Meghalaya, the Abode of Clouds, home of the Khasi, in the country of India (the land sloping and fairway-green; what I think Ireland must look like), there are five black pigs. Four piglets and a sow; a small number, but still. Pigs with a sour smell. Pigs who sleep clumped together. Pigs who are unabashed, putting soul and body into eating, making catastrophic outrageous eating sounds, while at the Jesuit hut the young meditators recite the Angelus. *And the word was made flesh ... and dwelt among us ...* as the pigs flail into their food, attacking with duty and glee, as if they've been training for this moment all their lives.

I sit often with the pigs, look at them, and touch the bristle of hair. They seem to make the most sense. I've never been around pigs much.

The pigs are tended by Jesuit novices from tribes all over northeast India. Khasi, Garo, Bodo, Adivasi, Naga, Maw. Some of these tribes are enemies of each other. Except for occasional anguished moments in volleyball, they all seem to get along here.

The novices run everywhere and sing blood-drenched Protestant songs and bow low before the holy sacrament when it comes out of its gold casement. On the front of the altar is the paper cutout of a chalice. It is taped to the altar cloth, colored with a yellow marker. If I had any remaining hesitation about the authentic worshiping credentials of this place, this chalice obliterated it. Like the pictures on the cardboard box that Philip of Toronto kneels before, it is another icon I think I could stare at all day long.

The tabernacle where the host lives is a miniature bamboo church with four panes of yellow glass and a thatched roof lit by a soft green bulb. Outside the chapel that houses the miniature chapel I sit on cement that the novices laid two years ago. I listen as Lucky Henry pronounces his words with a fierce precision, as if his Jesuit calling depends on it. I correct him. Make him repeat. Later, he talks about how his people, the Maw, are different from the people of this region, the Khasi. How the Maw eat the passion fruit which grows everywhere in the forests. It grows everywhere because the Maw eat it and then they go to the toilet in the forests—everywhere and anywhere. And the seeds of the passion fruit are in what they expel on the ground, and then they grow into the fruit.

Reifying and Repudiating

THERE IS A SCHOOL OF THOUGHT within Mahayana Buddhism called *Madhyamika*—the middle way. This school declares that all of reality, everything that is, may be looked at through two perspectives: conventional and ultimate. A snake on the ground viewed through the lens of conventional reality is there. The serpent is not simply an illusion, an airy vision of nothingness, the usual image of Buddhist thought. It is not mist in the form of a snake that you can put your hand through. The snake is a thing to be dealt with. It coils, moves, flickers its tongue, stops you in a school yard. It will bite you if you touch it.

Viewed through the perspective of ultimate reality, that same snake, even though we can see and touch it, is not actually there. Ultimately, the snake has no existence.

One and the same snake can be approached in two ways. In *Madhyamika* thought, there is no distinction between these ways. Conventional reality (*samvritamatra*) is bound up with ultimate reality (*paramarthasatya*). Conventionally, a thing is seen as existing, although ultimately that thing does not exist. It would be impossible for someone to declare that a thing called "snake" ultimately had no existence, if one could not even see that snake conventionally. Ultimate reality is absolutely rinsed into conventional reality, like colored dye into a piece of fabric.

It is a strange thing to consider and, if you subscribe to this philosophy, it can throw you into uncertainty. Depending how you look at it, a thing does exist, and that same thing does not exist.

You could say this *Madhyamika* view of reality goes against what is known as "the principle of non-contradiction." This declares that two contradictory things cannot be true at the same time. It cannot be both 4:00 PM and 4:27 PM in Omaha at the same time. A car cannot be a car and a pigeon. A snake cannot both exist and not exist.

And yet, following the train of *Madhyamika* thought, it can be 4:00 PM and 4:27 PM, a car can be a pigeon, and a snake can both exist and not exist.

Taking such a view of things, this precarious interplay between two states of being, this brazenly driving a stake into the heart of the principle of non-contradiction, decenters you. It throws you off balance. If you are a *bodhisattva*, a Buddhist student on the path toward enlightenment, it prevents you from thinking that you have it all figured out; that you have a clear fix on what it means to say that a thing exists; that you can know something when, in fact, you cannot.

In the dialogues of Plato, his protagonist Socrates declares that he is the wisest person in Athens, because he knows that he knows nothing. His fellow citizens think they know, but actually they do not. It is clear to Socrates that he himself really doesn't know anything, which is his true wisdom.

Socrates would question his companions about what they thought was true. Perhaps they believed it was true that "Pegasus is not a bird" (they never would have talked about this). Socrates humbly asks questions of his "interlocutor," or conversation partner, one after another after another. What makes a bird, what makes a horse? Where did you learn what you know, where did they learn what they know, and what if a bird is not a bird? Socrates poses questions that eventually get the man to contradict himself. The Socratic method, employed by Socrates. Socrates is leading his conversation partner toward a truth that the man has not yet grasped. The truth, namely, that he does not yet have knowledge, but is in ignorance.

Eventually, the interlocutor does not even know what he thinks or believes. Everything he thought he knew about wing and beast is shot to pieces. He is delivered into *aporia*, a state of intellectual confusion, his mind out of sorts. Its usual channels have collapsed. This sense of "no answers" can keep one humble, away from fixed notions of "grasping" truth, containing reality.

For the *bodhisattva*, not trying to grasp reality is the path to reality. Truth comes to him when he realizes he can't fully know truth; when he acknowledges that what seems to be is not always what is. This is the blessed grail, the sacred saffron fleece of the *bodhisattva*: to live in a place of not-grasping—not grasping at what he thinks is real. Some call this humility.

THE WORLD CLEARLY was not made for Carrie because it couldn't keep her alive past the age of eighteen. But suddenly, the world opens up because she has left it. Carrie has left the world of conventional reality, you might say, her body no longer walking the planet, and she lives in its ultimate reality. Her spirit soars, invisible. And now she can experience more of conventional reality than she ever could while she was alive in conventional reality. She went to all the places on earth she ever wanted to visit! Suddenly, it is reversed! The grand breadth of the world, it would seem, is suddenly made for Carrie. It is more-available to Carrie, passed, than to her classmate Shaina, living. Carrie dies and she has, if nothing else, a far more interesting experience in the material world visiting, say, the Taj Mahal, than Shaina will in any conventional welcome-week mixer. What do we really know about the lives and journeys of these two girls, or about anyone?

WHO GRACIOUSLY FUNDS the institutions that help the poor, bolster the arts, and build our common sense of social purpose? Financial titans who create economies that create the poor, that shred beauty, that rip apart our sense of social purpose; executives who pay a minimal wage to confect an entire population of an underclass they end up supporting; corporations that fight tooth and nail against the scaffolding of equity that would render their own philanthropy unneeded.

In the religious world, we bow and scrape before the affluent to fund charities their own politics help create the need for.

"The poor exist for the sake of the rich and the rich exist for the sake of the poor," writes Joe Heschmeyer. "Together we can grow in charity, and draw each other closer to heaven."

You want insanity, picture perfect? Here it is. I sleep under a freeway so you can get to heaven. Be not fooled dear friend, it's fundamentally not true.

And yet, principle of non-contradiction, it is true. Because charity can build virtue, and receiving charity can, well, keep you alive.

It is an awful and insane thing to own up to, such rigged economic arrangements, even if our entire lives agitate against it. It is baffling and throws us off kilter, the world's reliance on sacred financial excess. It creates confusion, *aporia*, the world is wholly wrong, it makes no sense.

And it throws us back to something bigger than us, a Power whose stock-in-trade is to rip apart all certainties and remind us that *we don't know*. Who takes us out of the fires of the mind and delivers us to the place of No Sense. Where, one moment, the Lord invites us to rail against a tech magnate for how he runs his company, and the other, to let him finance our Catholic charities.

And is it okay to do this? Well? You hesitate? No clear answer?

The fourth-century Buddhist teacher, Asanga, says that, when looking at reality, a *bodhisattva* needs to beware the temptation of either "reifying" or "repudiating." Reifying is declaring that the world is entirely there. Everything is what it appears to be, concrete, able to be touched. All is wholly and entirely conventional reality—the snake is real.

Repudiation declares nothing is there, nothing exists. The world is only ultimate reality. In the final analysis, no snakes.

But, according to Asanga and *Madhyamika* thought in general, it is not okay to do only one or the other, reify or repudiate. The world ought to be seen through the lens of both conventional and ultimate reality. We ought not to make them two distinct things. We have to accept that the world—life itself, you might say—contradicts itself. Things indeed are both there and not there.

Asanga declared that it is the refusal to reify and repudiate, and instead take the middle path, that gets one to reality, to a state of non-grasping, to being like Socrates, who was okay with knowing what he didn't know.

We live here and we see through a glass darkly. We can touch things, we can deal with life, but we can't know fully how we ought to handle the pleasure and attrition that living entails. What, ultimately, do we know? What can we really grasp about what exactly God is doing?

Helena in *A Midsummer Night's Dream* says love looks not with the eyes but with the mind. Trying to create a God who operates in a way that makes sense to us, a divinity who works like other people work: a branch manager, a shortstop, an actuary, a salesman. The Almighty probably cannot be fixed like that. What was Willy Loman selling anyway? *No one knows.* And we're all in that theater, watching that wrenching play, all the time.

This is maybe crushingly obvious, that God's ways are so far above our ways. Jews and Christians, at least, are aware of this and have been from the get-go. That God is ultimately a vast mystery to us. That really we don't know what is going on.

But maybe the reason to bring up this Eastern philosophy, the more comforting notion, here, when it comes to life and suffering, reality and unreality, making and unmaking, is that even Buddhists don't always know what's going on.

THEN THE LORD told the frightened prophet to scale the mountain and the Lord with dispatch would appear. And a terrible wind came unto that place and crushed the rocks, now pebbles, now sand, but the Lord was not there. The earth shook, fire blazed, entire woodlands and watersheds and the Lord was in neither.

And after the fire, a voice so light it could not be heard and was heard.

It is said such a faint sound is enough to live by.

In the Garden of the Central American Martyrs

I SIT IN A SMALL ROOM in a cheap hotel with an old grandmother in a blue dress. She has poor eyesight and cannot see the television well, so she listens to the radio. Her granddaughter Olga and I are there, at the Happy House Hotel, to bring her communion. We have walked nearly an hour to get here from San Antonio Abad on the hill down to this hotel near the center of San Salvador. It is hot out and the grandmother is weary and complains that her food has no taste. This is distressing because she was one of those souls who helped start base communities in the Jesuit parish of San Antonio Abad in the 1980s. Base communities are collections of people who read the gospels together and talk about the struggles in their country. They see fit to put one into the other, the gospel and crude reality, and see what can be done. They were vital to everything that made the country what it was, and at the very least their elderly founders ought to have food that tastes like something.

The oldness of this woman, her small room, her blue dress, her beautiful legacy of confronting her people's *realidad*, the quiet words I can barely understand, all the final consonants dropped. What do we do with such a woman?

We sit and talk, the three of us. Olga and I met at mass a couple of weeks before this. We do not have much in common except that we are both Catholic. I can barely understand the language and it is hot out and the grandmother, Gloria, has *presence*. So much presence it is almost difficult to be around her.

Salvador. El Salvador. Who wants to hear about El Salvador? Surely there will be distressing talk of poverty and deployments and sexual violence against religious women. Who wants to hear about one more nun taken away and dealt with in such a manner? When I hear the name *El Salvador*, I drift back some years and see a map of a small country in the corner of a news broadcast and something about troop levels and containment policy and fighting in the city.

When I hear *El Salvador*, I glimpse a silver steel plate. Something to do with the letters *lv* in the word "*Salvador.*" Letters that are sharp, letters that slice. I hear *El Salvador*, and I see a steel plate cutting into something, and a dark helicopter hovering over green trees. For some people, Salvador is just a special cordoned-off zone for teeing up new energy to hate Ronald Reagan. A place down there that has war and rice and beans and *pupusas* and the sweet Spanish language. A place where six Jesuit academics were shot in a garden in the night. And Romero, the bishop. We went to the church where he too was taken out, and pictures of the blood spilling down his face.

There was mass at the Jesuit University of Central America, the UCA—a lovely crowded campus with twenty-year-olds in shining garb. The graves of the Jesuit professors in a crypt in the church. A poster of another beloved Jesuit who died but wasn't killed, just died. He received the Sword of Ignatius a week before he died. "That's a stupid award," a classmate says. "Didn't Ignatius lay down his sword at Manresa? Jon Cortina worked for peace and non-violence. It's a stupid award to give someone."

This is the good place to be, Salvador and all that it sounds like. The good hard tragic place. The cross with the blood still on it. Salvador's bright cloth for export seems to be such a cross, such violence. In other countries in Latin America, the people have more profound fabrics, patterned garments, sublime treasures, mysterious ancient colonies, quirky knick-knacks. Things you can buy and sell to remember the country. Salvador has some of those too, but I think that mostly Salvador has the blood of its people and the way they erase each other from existence.

This didn't just take place in the civil war of the 1980s, I am told. There were the thirty thousand killed in the army massacre of 1932 following a peasant uprising. It was an event that seems to have been some kind of turning point, a fastening of an attitude, a hunch in the shoulders, a low dark note in the music played at mass, even the joyous entrance songs. Another American Jesuit working here wonders out loud if 1932 still lives in the people. The people who saw that, when they organized, they would be met with brutal and overwhelming force; a people who let go. After 1932, traditional ways and garb and the Nahuatl language were abandoned. As the Salvadoran poet, Roque Dalton, writes:

We were all born half dead in 1932
we survived but only half alive
each shouldering the weight of thirty thousand
    dead
with growing interest
and returns

We Jesuit language students visit a small mountain town where the government dug a mass grave to deal with the residue of 1932. This town, we are told, has been a particularly hard place ever since: divided, angry, and violent. I reject that the town is this way, consider it over-dramatic.

Then I wonder: if my own history held the murder of everyone in my family, and maybe everyone I ever knew, would that make me a little fearful? And my children, wouldn't they see that fear, and wouldn't it sink into them, burrow into their bones? And my children's children?

Or would they reject that fear utterly and live, somehow, in the opposite direction. Living with a stupid boldness. Casting aside all caution. Taking up the political party of no fear; pretending as if there is nothing in the world to be vigilant about. Either way, because they care too much or care too little—living with fear or with reckless anger—they are being controlled by some outside force. So, in this town that lives above the mass grave of the risen up and slaughtered, there are, today, parties of hard right (keep the military in charge) and hard left (keep in power the militia of my ideals), and few in between. This is sterling evidence of a culture whose goodness remains hovering all around them, unclaimed, afraid.

But then someone else tells me it wasn't the 1980s or 1932, it was always this way in Salvador. At least since Spain conquered the Indians five hundred years ago and reorganized the economy, controlled what the peasants produced, and controlled everything else about them. Ever since then, the people have been lashing out at each other.

There are countries in Latin America much poorer than El Salvador, but in 2006, virtually no place is more violent. The most recent civil war officially ended fifteen years earlier, but the war has simply gone underground. It has fragmented itself and dispersed into pockets and channels, the killings in this new war popping up here and there, day after day, in what is called crime. In the United States, our teachers inform us, there are six murders per one hundred thousand people; in Salvador there are forty-one. Apart from those places caught up in declared wars, few countries in the world are deadlier than El Salvador. (And today, fourteen years later, the violence continues unabated, driving terrorized people up to American borders, and everyone's tale-tell reactions to that.)

But all of this is wrong too. Salvador is not just the killings, the history of oppression, and whatever else a visiting language student wants it to be. It is everything everyone is: friendly, conservative, radical, clammed up, delightful, sinful, beautiful, complicated, with statues of dead men no one looks at, flurries of soccer bursting up in hard-baked open lots, populated by holy men and women, even when no one is trying to kill them. At a grand theater complex, I saw *The Return of Superman*. He was awkward and stupendous as ever.

Still, it is the unpleasant side you remember. It is this desolation that you have bowed your head before—the unpleasant stats, the images of death, the rose gardens of torture, the poverty and sickness, the facts and figures of all these hard things from way back until now. A man comes onto a city bus in San Salvador, fixes his feet in the aisle, braces himself, fiercely plays guitar, blows into wooden pipes, sings a wailing song, smiles and walks down the aisle holding out his hand. The whole thing feels panicked. Where are the wife and child tucked away behind that song? When I gave him money, he gave me a red sucker shaped like a toothbrush that lit up. It was the worst candy I'd ever had in my life. I can still taste it now, several years later, just thinking about it. All the worse because it was shaped like a toothbrush, and had a light in it.

The Brazilian bishop Dom Helder Camara is quoted on pamphlets and tracts saying, "*When I feed the poor they call me a saint. When I ask, 'Why are there poor?' they call me a communist.*" Why indeed are there poor? Let us go forth, let us sound out the underlying structures of poverty, the why of injustice. Isn't this one of our core competencies, we Jesuits? Given its history, Salvador seems to be the right place for all of this—religious men hot on the trail of some great wrong gratefully walking in this place and feeling these lingering waves of holy suffering.

BRIAN AND I ARE SITTING on a bench in the dark in the town of Perquin, in the northeast hills of El Salvador, watching *The Passion of the Christ*. The town square is ringed with lighted booths selling *pupusas*, funnel cakes, bootleg CDs, T-shirts featuring Oscar Romero or Che

Guevara. There is some noise coming from these booths, set up for the Perquin winter festival, but in the square itself it is mostly quiet. Children, mothers, old men, and we two Jesuits watch this movie in the warm air. We watch as soldiers whip Jesus. The scene goes on for several brutal minutes, Christ beaten viciously, over and over and over, by grunting thick-necked men, ebullient in their sport.

It is painful to watch, and when the film was released in 2004, this part had many detractors. What galvanized critics wasn't solely a fear that the movie would renew old anti-Semitic, "Christ-killer" feelings. It was the brutality of scenes like this one. The suffering of the Lord is taken too far, its depiction misguided. In the whipping scene, Mel Gibson is simply making Jesus into a tough guy who can take anything you dish out. The soldiers are shown leaning over, gasping for breath, while Jesus manages to stand up one more time to take his punishment.

This scene, and the movie as a whole, give high regard to brutality and suffering. It steeps in the pools of blood, the special, precision quality of the Lord's agony. During the crucifixion his arm is pulled out of its socket. When the cross is raised and then dropped into place, Jesus's body is jarred inhumanly.

The Passion comes off as a solemn, reverse-action movie, one where the hero gets beaten up by all comers, doesn't fight back, and yet takes it with a fierce bravado. *Is this all you've got?*

I loved the movie. But it placed too much emphasis on the physical courage of Christ. The movie's theology seemed to declare that life is a bloody, violent battle between forces of light and forces of darkness.

This theology, this outdated Christianity looks at the world too starkly, too simplistically. It is nothing but a gruesome focus on how much Jesus suffered for us and how we should be grateful to be allowed one sacred inch into the borders of his kingdom. The Stations of Light are nowhere in sight. The familiar Catholic drumbeat: it's all about suffering! The first part of being Christian: you don't deserve any bit of your life.

This is where religion is like a prod, urging us to meditate on Christ's poor wounded body and think on how sinful we and our world are; how we, each of us, have killed Jesus. The shame of our complicity should snap our lives back into a holy place.

We ought to be beyond this way of thinking. We should simply accept the love of God and let that fire every moment of our lives.

Earlier on the day they showed *The Passion*, Brian and I went down to the town of El Mozote. El Mozote is two bus rides from Perquin. It is a small village with few residents. It has a church, a few houses, a stand where women sell sodas and bean and cheese *pupusas*. Near the church, there is also a small wooden booth, unmanned except when visitors show up. When visitors arrive, a woman appears and tells you that, in early

December 1981, during the civil war, soldiers of the government army wiped out nearly the entire town of El Mozote. They slaughtered men, women, children—everyone they could find.

The massacre was carried out by the Atlacatl battalion, a special unit of the Salvadoran army, as part of a "scorched earth" raid, one intended not only to wipe out any guerillas, but to so terrify the people that no one would think of joining the insurgency. The soldiers rounded up people and shot them in a church, Mark Danner tells us. They grabbed men by the hair, pulled back their heads and cut them off with machetes. They chased women into the forest and shot them up and down. Soldiers strung ropes to trees and hung little children. They went into houses, grabbed girls clinging to their mothers, and took them away. Later, the girls' cries and screams could be heard in the dark hills as they were raped and then killed.

When the battalion finished off all the people, they slaughtered every cow, horse, goat, and pig and burned all the houses and many of the bodies. That night, people in the neighboring villages "saw thick columns of smoke rising from El Mozote, and smelled the odor of what seemed like tons of roasting meat."

The army and the government denied the massacre ever took place. It was passed off as a fantasy told by old women and encouraged by rebel sympathizers; a wild story intended to discourage the United States from continuing its funding of the Salvadoran army. The U.S. Congress was not swayed by old women and rebels. After declaring that the Salvadoran government was making progress in the area of human rights, America continued sending money. The serpent had ringed the grounds. No one was getting out.

Finally, in the early 1990s, after the signing of the peace accords between the guerillas and the army, what took place at El Mozote officially came to light. It was documented by the United Nations for exactly what it was.

So, when I sit in the town of Perquin and watch the scourging in *The Passion*, I realize that Mel Gibson's Catholicism is not really that outdated. What I'm watching makes a lot of sense.

Maybe Salvadorans would agree. They may see a scene like this as simply what happens. Christ is hauled away, ferociously beaten, over and over again, and then killed as barbarically as a man could possibly be. We know something about that. Our God went through what we went through. Is it so surprising, that they do this to him? That they take him out, to shut him up? To keep him from stirring the people into revolution, which will only bring down the fury of Rome on Israel? Is this so unexpected, that one is cut down, viciously, in the name of saving the many? We will meditate on Christ's poor, wounded, broken body, in the same way we looked on our countrymen, tortured, shot, burned; our kids swaying from trees.

The movie goes on. Jesus is put through his paces and then dies on the cross. Rain falls, thunder crashes. The pillars of the temple shake and the high priests are tossed around. Then, suddenly, in the square in Perquin, the sound cuts off and the screen goes black. After a minute or two, there is an announcement over the loudspeakers that the movie is finished.

We all sit there for a few moments, wondering if they really mean it. They didn't get to the resurrection. Finally, we get up and wander away. For a few minutes I think that the people showing the movie, for some reason, ended it this way on purpose.

Probably it was just some kind of electrical malfunction.

AND SO GLORIA. Her peasanthood, her dignified suffering, her people's history of being annihilated by special battalions. Beautiful and heroic. And all that presence that is difficult to be around. Presence you just can't take.

It is easy to be around the idea of peasant Gloria and difficult to be around the flesh and blood of her. She has a certain aura, gift-wrapped in that she can hardly see or hear and listens to the radio and has that blue dress and Olga, who brings her communion, and two grandsons in black who show up later with soup and tear off bits of tortilla to put into the soup and are mimes; mimes gesturing on the sidewalks and byways what is still wrong in their country.

It seems we should rejoice in this opportunity to be surrounded by all of this, but her presence and goodness are plain exhausting.

After delivering communion to Gloria, I walk home with Olga down the busted sidewalk, and I ask her where she works. She replies, from what my poor Spanish can gather, that she is employed by a German printing company. Instantly, I want to find out whether her company treats her well or not. I say to her, "*Tu compañia es buena?*"

Maybe I can strike up a conversation with Olga that will spark some awareness of how miserably she is being treated by these Alemanians. This conversation could be the tiny little spark that would lead to a minor revolution among the clerical class of foreign-owned printing companies. An uprising that may lead to others. A small step, but a step, toward a revolution that will not be met like 1932 was; nor carried out with guns and rocket launchers as in the 1980s. One that will play out much, much differently; a sideways response to El Mozote and all those other horrors. Maybe our little walk home will be more than just a walk home.

Perhaps that is why it is difficult to be with old and poor Gloria or most anyone else here. Because, in these instances, we visiting Jesuits are not doing anything about their poverty or their wars. We are not rooting out grave structural causes of injustice, subverting dominant paradigms, helping found base communities and searching the Bible for hints to a way out. We are not wearing black T-shirts and miming in the streets for justice. All this time we have not been part of changing anything here.

Yet with Olga maybe it will be different. Slowly, carefully, she and I can have a stilted conversation that will actually lead somewhere. A small clearing etched into the dark thicket of Salvador's history. "*Tu compañia es buena?*"

EVEN BUDDHISTS—Mahayanist of the *Madhyamika* school, or any school really—struggle to live in reality. Buddhists, and pretty much everyone with blood in their veins, reifies and repudiates. We tighten a false explanatory band around that which is too painful to bear (her breast cancer was God's plan, the priest told me so, end of story and now I'll go ahead shut down my emotions for the next twenty-five years). Or we sink into a deep despair about the entire project (her death was born of no plan—none we can see, and none we can't see—and hope is a thing with vicious wings I'll contemplate no further).

We reify, crystalize with swift fury, our pain into something concretely meaningful or so help us God. *Clearly the Aqedah is a bromide against child sacrifice. Onto the next theodicy.* Or we repudiate, we cast from the realm of all possibility that any meaning could be sought deep in the tissues of this tragedy. *Apparently another name for God is Heavenly Infanticide. Charming.* And so we write off the whole project of God.

But if you avoid reifying and repudiating, if your run-of-the-mill *bodhisattva* allows for a certain kind of "unknowing," if she stops trying to get a clear fix on what is the what, if she wrestles with the Aqedahs that come her way as they sit on the page instead of hastily explaining them away, she may, eventually, end her suffering.

Life is suffering, said Sakyamuni Buddha. The First Noble Truth. Life is *dukkha*, unsatisfactory, flawed. Located in *samsara*, the cycle of continuous life/death/rebirth, the dreary round and round; existence is a repository of human pain and frustration.

The Second Noble Truth explains where suffering comes from. Said the Buddha to the Fortunate Five, his first disciples, "The origination of suffering is the thirst for further existence, which comes along with pleasure and passion and brings passing enjoyment here and there."

This suffering, as John Strong puts it, is "a thirst that we cannot assuage, a clinging to possessions, to persons, to life itself."

The Third Noble Truth is that there is a way to end suffering: namely, by stopping our grasping. "With elimination of craving, the suffering that originates from it will cease without remainder," says the Buddha.

We move toward ending suffering by a practice of learning to see things not as we would like to see them, but as they actually are: impermanent, deficient, to be detached from. All things are ultimately unsatisfying.

In Buddhist thought, this fundamental nature of all things is *sunyata*—"emptiness." All is empty, nothing ultimately has substance. There is nothing in the world that can sustain and, so to speak, refresh you in the deepest part of your soul. Grasping at things, clinging to the stuff of life—health, possessions, sensual pleasures—is ultimately a fool's game because these things are ultimately empty.

As John of the Cross writes: "To reach satisfaction in all, desire satisfaction in nothing. To come to possess all, desire the possession of nothing. To arrive at being all, desire to be nothing. To come to the knowledge of all, desire the knowledge of nothing. . . ."

It is about not trying to control your life, but about letting go. "Nothing prisons the truth so quickly," says Christian Wiman, "as an assurance that one has found it."

This letting go of craving in order to end suffering and get to *nirvana* is a practice. As taught by the Buddha in the Fourth Noble Truth, we practice this letting go by living out a set of principles called the Eightfold Path. This path entails right views, right intentions, right speech, right action, right livelihood, right effort, right mindfulness, and right concentration. It is a way of life that helps one stay in deeper reality, not chasing the thin baubles of empty reality that flit and flicker through life.

THE *BHAGAVAD GITA*, a dialogue in which the spirit of the god Krishna urges the warrior Arjuna to join a great battle, throws light on pursuing what is real and avoiding what is not:

From the world of the senses, Arjuna, comes heat and comes cold, and pleasure and pain. They come and they go: they are transient. Arise above them strong soul. The man whom these cannot move, whose soul is one, beyond pleasure and pain, is worthy of life in Eternity. The unreal never is: the Real never is not. This truth indeed has been seen by those who can see the true.

Krishna goes on to discuss the desires—"disordered attachments"—that block one from the true:

It is greedy desire and wrath, born of passion, the great evil, the sum of destruction: this is the enemy of the soul. All is clouded by desire: as fire by smoke, as a mirror by dust, as an unborn babe by its covering. Wisdom is clouded by desire, the ever present enemy of the wise, desire in its innumerable forms, which like a fire cannot find satisfaction.

In *Madhyamika* thought, ending suffering by coming to the truth that all things are empty means encountering life through the lens of conventional reality as much as possible. It entails going forthrightly through as the way to *nirvana*. The only way to enlightenment is not by avoiding life and its diamond-sharp edges, but by dealing with life exactly as it is. Getting to *nirvana*, in other words, is not flying away from the senses. A *bodhisattva* does not leave the world behind, she finds *nirvana* when she mixes and mingles precisely where she is. It is not about escaping things, but about having a right relationship with them. The only way out is to stay right in it. Living in the pain of reality is where she finds refuge for her soul.

GRACIAS, says Olga.

You pause. *Gracias*? Excuse me? You ask how her awful and oppressive German company is and she smiles and says *Gracias*?

Then you realize what you have done. You have not stressed enough *buena*, have not given it an upward swing, to make your sentence a question. So it has remained as it is, a declarative statement: "*Tu compañia es buena.*"

And so, instead of asking the question that might one day stir up wave after wave of striking office clerks that will root out the evil coursing through Olga's country, that will implant in Salvadoran souls once and for all the idea that God is active and alive and deals out justice like ringing a bell, rather than do all that, you have merely affirmed this woman's companionship: "Your company is good." And Olga, pleased, says "*Gracias.*"

So you start trying to say in Spanish, "No, no, your company, how is your *company*? How is the *corporation* that you work for, their *labor policies*. Do they treat their workers with any sense of . . . ?"

But you trail off before you can get any of this out. Instead you reply, "*Sí, sí.*" You pause, and then say, again, quietly, "*Sí.*" You walk down the street with her, a little base community of two, and then the two of you part toward your separate homes. Apparently, the universe did not need you to reify Olga's struggle in any way, but just to notice she was there, and what it was like.

Lo, the Devil!

IN *THE SCREWTAPE LETTERS*, C. S. Lewis warns us to think about the devil neither too much nor too little, this one who comes in many guises and leads us to the edge of hopelessness, if not to that promised land itself. Is the devil (The devil! Such a word! It is quaint, it is adorable!), is this one ultimately responsible for tragedy and heartache and pain, for all our boys in juvy? Do we indict on behalf of our twelve-year-old inmates neither schools nor cops nor a housing crisis nor family nor the second amendment nor the legacy of slavery nor the dismantling of the manufacturing base in Midwestern American cities but a spirit so wicked as to be nearly invisible and completely under the radar of any proper sociological study? Do we accuse, as Ignatius and others name him, the Enemy?

Lo, the devil! Behold, the Enemy! It can work through anything and everything! The old ways! Let us not forget the old ways!

Come, you dread American sinners, we might say, who piled up absurd amounts of wealth buying and selling American picket-fence dreams in such insanely convoluted fashion that it eventually created a sinister house of tissue paper just waiting for the smallest breath to blow up the American economy—mad financial schemes that may still be operating now.

You, who have fallen under the spell of the Dark Angel, sell all you have! Sell it and do not give the money to the poor. You do not exist for their sake nor do they for yours. Burn your cash in a heap, throw it in the sewer, afford yourselves no tender feelings of paying for poor men's wells, their community centers, their battles with malaria, or their "brick-and-mortar" school campaigns. Cast your lucre in a kiln and follow these kids into jail. Confession and penance are the only thing that will save you. What better place to begin than the solitude of a state or federal anchorage?

All of you, whitewashed tombs, smart, industrious, "world-disrupting" on the outside but inside filled with hypocrisy and evil-doing; enter into our blessed cell with all the other charmers, smug saviors, and disciples of half-truths. Think on your sins and beg mercy from the Lord.

We might cry out all these things because Lucifer (good word, Lucifer!) has gathered all these men and women into his sweet arms. He has entered their souls like an angel of light, as Ignatius would put it, bringing them attractive, pleasant thoughts about their good deeds and hearty ways of life, about returns for shareholders and traditional American go-getting. Then, little by little, he entices them over to his own hidden deceits and evil intentions.

Evil, sin, minions of the dark prince. The old ways still hold!

All this corruption starts small, of course. Begins with the barely noticeable sins. The ones like pebbles the thirsty crow drops into the quarter-filled pitcher. Enough water rises up, and somehow keeps rising, that it overflows the pitcher and eventually floods the room. The sins can start anywhere. On a soccer field, for instance, where a woman once battled for her soul.

For a few Wednesdays one summer, Marney Cray played soccer in a university stadium with a small group of men—grad students, researchers, young professors— a short field, and small goals on the east end of the stadium near the red cinder track. One player who showed up two or three times was an eighty-two-year-old man. An eighty-two-year-old guy! He was on the field, he was running around, he was playing soccer with twenty- and thirty-year-olds. He was fifty years older than everyone else! This was awesome! He ran, he passed, he shot, his hair was darker than it should have been and no matter. The old man was out there!

During one of these games, Marney had the ball and this man defended her and Marney tried to get around him. He was between Marney and the sweet-looming goal.

At this point you should know that, in soccer, to "nutmeg" someone means to pass the ball through his legs. It is a rare and wonderful move to get around a defender. I have no idea why it is called a nutmeg. It embarrasses the opponent and brings glory to the one who "megs." It is, in certain sporting circles, one of the most joyous things a human can accomplish.

So, Marney and the old man. His stiff legs were spread about two feet apart. There it was. You see where this is going. It was there for the taking. The rare and precious opportunity. Marney pushed the ball through his legs, went around him and gathered it on the other side. She nutmegged an eighty-two-year-old man.

Immediately, Marney realized what she had done. The old man clapped for her. He clapped for Marney! And not sarcastically. Jesus Lord!

Marney's sin is ever before her, her pride is before her, and Lord have mercy. God created a human who could do such a thing.

Clearly, this sin is not God's fault. It is all on Marney. She passed that ball. She wanted so badly to score, to look good in the eyes of the other players, to show up the cocky men, that she made a fool of an old man, a feeling that immediately ricocheted back to her. Pride! So much pride, to win no matter the cost!

In truth, Marney's culpability would not be so great. It was not a mortal sin (grave matter, full knowledge, deliberate consent). It was a lesser offense, unplanned, venial. I am not certain it was even a sin. But such acts weaken charity. "Deliberate and unrepented venial sin disposes one little by little to commit mortal sin" (*CCC*, Part 3, Article 8, Number 1863).

If only Marney would give herself to God. It is all on her to give all of her to God. If only she would rest securely in the Lord, then she would be much more humble and wouldn't need to prove herself to any group of glory-days' athletes.

And if only Marney's family had taught her well enough, she would not have done this thing. And if only her elders had taught her family true kindness and restraint, it would have filtered down and reached her and she would never have done such a thing. And if only someone had indoctrinated humility into her elders' elders, their ancestor's ancestors, and all the way down the ages to the very first couple and God their first great Teacher, then such a thing would not have happened on that soccer field.

God created humans weak enough to fall to pride, which would filter down through the glaciers and form a sediment that would become one day a low valley, a sheer outcropping, a deep red canyon filled with young women carrying out deplorable soccer tricks against eighty-two-year-olds who clap for them with no irony.

As surely as unchecked avarice can crush an economy, the legacy of a nutmeg is buried deep in our bones. God let us have a gene to be this kind of unlovely people.

And even the incarnation, God ripped into the shroud of earth and indicted with weakness and sweat and redemption, does not wipe it out. The Son of God did not die and rise powerfully enough, with a final and complete supply of salvation to destroy our most evil tendencies while we yet walk the earth.

The incarnation does not seal your viciousness behind a wall forever so it can never come out. Nor does the incarnation wrap you up in its woolen cowl and keep you from being wounded by other people's sins. A shoot has sprung from the stump of Jesse, from his roots a bud has blossomed, and still the poor are not judged with justice, nor are the ruthless struck with the rod of his mouth. The ruthless keep bearing down. The appearance of God-made-man does not keep us from getting hammered by life again and again.

God actually sent his son, Light from Light, into the world to show everyone how to live. If that is the case, why indeed are we the way we are? We have no excuses. The incarnation makes our bad behavior an even worse thing. It only reveals all the more starkly the void between who we are and who we ought to be. He showed us, he laid it out, paving stone by stone. Then he suffered, died, rose, and we still can't get it right? We humiliate old men on soccer fields and far worse.

Original sin? Shall we go that route? Write your dissertation, lay out your case, root yourself in the Tradition. Of course, we have our leanings, always our vile leanings. Who would disagree? We are fundamentally askew. Man was tempted in the garden, stopped trusting God, and disobeyed God's chief command. And, except apparently for Abraham, we have been disobeying ever since. This doctrine of original sin is the reason not even Christ's redemption wipes away our freedom to do the wrongs we tend to do.

But how much iniquity can we lay upon the sturdy plank of original sin until even it collapses? Until not even original sin can serve as an excuse or reason for so much human wrongdoing, so much pathetic indifference?

Christians today, or least those in the West, sometimes blame the general badness of the world on all the people who have abandoned the faith, or never really took it seriously; those who live counter to the Way, or the philosophies and movements that render Christ and God an afterthought. Christians blame René Descartes, Immanuel Kant, the Enlightenment, Industrialism, Modernism, unrestrained sexual license. We call out Frederick Nietzsche, V. I. Lenin, Charles Darwin, the breakdown of morals, the death of school prayer, the liberated homosexual, the destruction of the family; Capitalism, Marxism, McCarthyism, the splitting of the atom, Gloria Steinem, Harry Blackmun. We harangue creeping relativism, Islamist extremism, and rampant secularism.

In fact, we ought to consider whether the fault lies not in these stars but in our own Christian selves. Is it really entirely "their fault" that people just won't accept or live the true Christian message? Or is it we who have made Christianity anything but credible?

God knows those boys in Minneapolis are there. He knows the jails are there, waiting to swallow them up. What is he doing about it? *He sent us*, the story goes. God has given those kids "you and me" to do something about it. God, through secondary causality, has fashioned the template of the solid family unit, the supportive extended community, and of course, the full program of the Christian faith and its most complete iteration in the Roman Catholic Church and all its affiliates—all of this to keep these kids on the right side of jail. And still, they go there in devastating numbers. Well? Where are the saved Christians? Where is God? Where is anyone?

THERE IS WORK on the grounds in Kohima. They have nearly eighty acres and use about ten. Boniface, broad-shouldered and ever-smiling, has planted about twenty lemon and orange trees and one hundred more are on the way. With the novices, he has planted sixty guava plants, six apple trees, twelve peach trees, six apricot trees, two mango trees, twelve pear trees, fifteen hundred pineapple plants, eighty kilograms of ginger roots, which he will double. He's got a scattering of maize, beans, brinjal (basically, eggplant), capsicum, and squash. There are five avocado trees, ten banana trees, and some trees just for timber.

They care for the four piglets and a sow. "Yorkshires," Boniface tells me, and I nod, as if that means something to me. There are also fifty laying hens, ten rabbits, four hundred fingerlings in the pond, and three other ponds, finished or still being dug. "I like bodies of water," Boniface says. One is just for fish. As with the novices, there is so much potential out here. Potential food, ready to become its full self. *Dunamis* moving toward *hexis*, as Aristotle would put it, and points beyond. There is an overwhelming amount of food growing in this land. Nutrition and sustenance rising all around us.

The living and working quarters are four bamboo buildings, with corrugated metal roofs and sandbags on top to keep them in place. The buildings all have cement floors. There is one satellite TV in the dining room that the men crowd around to watch for half an hour after dinner. About five hundred yards up the hill the workers are constructing the new novitiate that will house forty Jesuits. More than a hundred men are there, mixing sand, breaking rocks, pounding nails.

I have it in me to make this one of those straight-shooting narratives baked into conventional reality answering bluntly the grand life question about "How Everyone Should Live." That this is a very acceptable and happy way to address all the heart-rending stories of the world, this little paradise in India. See how these men do! Look at the simplicity! Look at the capsicum! Behold the quiet bows every morning, the chickens skittering down the path, the silence at meals, and the prayer walks at night. The Five Keys to Jesuit Non-Intrusive Evangelization and Inculturation. Repeat! Repeat! A label wrapped on a bottle: "Our Way of Proceeding" is to go in and ask the people what they need. Invite them to name their deepest desires. And we help them attain those desires. To build schools, medical clinics, micro-credits.

Look how we do.

Oh, there is quite easily within me something so programmatic. Look, look here! The bloody and outdated Sacred Heart, it still works! It can work for you! Here! Here is the answer! There is in me something that wants to boil all of this down, fix it into a pamphlet.

Take every steely word by the novice master and every heavy breath by a dark-haired Maw doing pushups at 5:30 in the gray morning and fix it in the reader's waiting soul. Trot out each article of damp clothing hanging from a clothesline and getting rained on; every earnest smile, and all the dirty 1980s rock T-shirts; each encounter with Satan in the trembling first week of the Spiritual Exercises; all the tiny fish growing new scales in a rainwater pond; the thick weeds chopped by hand, the voices rising through the bamboo walls, the scraping of tin plates, the murmur of night prayer, the taking of vows, the sending forth throughout the valleys, to live Christ, start schools, fight for the poor.

I could condense it all and wrap it up in a slender package to disseminate to the four corners of the earth. I could do all that.

Because this was important and meaningful and the point of this Jesuit summer immersion, learning how to be sparkling missionaries with great dreams and how all this was the sign of God's beautiful presence in a harsh world. I could go on about this, I could.

But I think I'd rather talk about the pigs. I mean, who wouldn't?

The Moth II: A Fable

A ND THEN THERE WAS THE TIME when the moth got right
up in the dark lamp and singed itself, when any hint
of inner peace eroded and then simply vanished. A time
when the world called and the mind tunneled and God
indeed was distant, no matter how many times they say
God is so close. A time you brought on yourself and was
terribly brought on you.

There is not a lot more to say. You went down. There
were circumstances, place, and time. It doesn't really
matter what or how. The moment came.

Clearly, such a time was long in the making. The sudden kindling of darkness and sorrow, always ready at
hand. A night sitting with Jae on that sad mattress deep
in the city pleading not for sex but for a saturation of
love; wrapping her light brown arms around you as if
something inside her bones and skin could deliver grace.

Grace that would release whatever lower spirit had taken root that night and would not leave, no matter what you tried.

You have heard of John of the Cross. You know that when we suffer God is drawing us in close. So near to the shadow of him that we can't see anything at all for the darkness of his love. What John does not mention is that some people—and you were one of them—want only to run out of this shadow to the light of something evil called happiness. If there is a devil, and there is, he lives in the pitch-dark recesses of the mind spreading no hope more and more completely, with great and singular devotion.

Later someone told you, "Now you can really begin to pray."

Someone else said: "God can understand, He's been through that stuff too. It isn't that He sat up above and rode it out."

You began to talk to people, a few, as if you were talking for the first time.

And you remained in awe at the depths to which you went and for stretches at a time still could go.

Cade

O N THE BACK OF A T-SHIRT at a high school wrestling match in Custer, South Dakota:

> A golden heart stopped beating
> hard working hands put to rest
> God broke our hearts
> to prove to us
> he only takes the very best
> Cade: 2002
> 160 lbs: Regional champ

God took Cade. God swiped this child because he wants to surround himself with the finest out there.

Does God really...? How could a loving...? Did Cade actually want...? Answer the questions.

But the fact is God took Cade, no more than 160 lbs., regional champ, trussed up in a short blue unitard, molded plastic headgear, straps down along the chin, a small boy in his orthodontic headgear scrambling around on a blue mat, because Cade was a very good wrestler and just a very fine kid. The Lord Almighty snatched him up because he wanted the very best.

And you and your highest sacred theology, your Aquinas, your Augustine, your John of the Cross, so much smarter than the rhymed doctrine of a white cotton T-shirt, can you explain it any better? God removes from life the best. The end.

A Practice

WHEN A STUDENT DEMANDED from Sakyamuni Buddha clear and certain knowledge about the architecture of all things, the Buddha told him a story about another man who wanted certain knowledge. According to the Buddha, this man had been shot by a poisoned arrow. His friends and kin brought a surgeon to treat him. And the wounded man insisted to everyone: "I will not let the surgeon pull out this arrow until I know whether the man who wounded me was a noble or a brahmin or a merchant or a worker... until I know the name and clan of the man who wounded me... until I know whether the bow that wounded me was a long bow or a crossbow ... until I know with what kind of sinew the shaft that wounded me was bound—whether that of an ox or a buffalo or a lion or a monkey...." Said the Buddha: "All this would still not be known to that man and meanwhile he would die."

It is not about knowing. It is not about an intellectual comprehension of all that is. The point is to practice. (Or in the case of the arrow, let one be practiced upon.) The point of the Eightfold Path is to stop trying to understand why you suffer. Instead it is to practice detaching, over and over, as the only way to end suffering.

For Christians, humans will always, in one fashion or another, suffer. No matter how well we practice, we will always be afflicted, broken, and will be until we attain the kingdom. You cannot end suffering. (You end suffering by dealing with suffering.)

You will never end your suffering, O baptized one. You quit your suffering by regarding your suffering. You cannot put suffering to rout! You put suffering to rout by confronting suffering. Suffering will always be there. Suffering scatters when you face your suffering. There is no way to extinguish suffering. The way you extinguish your suffering is by walking with others who suffer. We are all *Madhyamika*, gleefully destroying principles of non-contradiction.

Here it is before me, this affliction. I cannot run from it, cannot excise it from my mind and body. What to do? The good *bodhisattva* acknowledges it, sizes it up, and tells the world that, yes, suffering has power over her. Names what afflicts her, and then names it again and yet again. Don't fight pain, she hears in the air, don't try to make something not so. Don't reify, don't repudiate. Surrender, Dorothy, my dear, surrender.

Exercises

I ONCE LIVED in a Jesuit community that employed a cook whose daughter cooked meals in another community on the same grounds. Everyone knew everyone. On the Fourth of July, our cook, the mother, made Rice Krispie treats that were green and pink and shaped like slices of watermelon. She put them out on the table in the dining room. Later, the priest in charge of food came into the kitchen through the dining room. The cook told him that she saw those treats in a recipe book and thought they looked cute.

"Do you think they're cute?" she asked him.

This priest paused and said quietly, yes, and then shortly left. Immediately, the mother called her daughter across the way. *He said they're cute*. As if the father had strolled into the dining room, seen the cookies incarnated on the counter, made haste into the hill country of the kitchen and said, "Those watermelon-shaped Rice Krispie treats are cute."

This priest is a kind and excellent guy who for years has served God and man faithfully and generously and has never in his entire life, I guarantee, stumbled upon any foodstuff anywhere and said it was cute. But when pressed about cute, he did say yes, and that was enough, and the word quickly got out.

The purpose of life according to Ignatius of Loyola is that *human beings are created to praise, reverence, etc.* He goes on audaciously to tell us how to do everything we will ever do.

> The other things on the face of the earth are created for the human beings, to help them in the pursuit of the end for which they are created. From this it follows that we ought to use these things to the extent that they help us toward our end, and free ourselves from them to the extent that they hinder us from it. To attain this it is necessary to. . . .

The instructions continue like this, plodding and unmystical. God's will for you, according to Ignatius, is knowable. It is not, as they say, so high in the sky that a twirling satellite has to be launched to bring it down to us. No, it is something very near, in your mouth and in your heart.

Ignatius created "spiritual exercises" whose goal, in the end, is to free ourselves from anything that keeps us from Christ. Not unlike Buddhism, this spirituality is about "clinging" to neither one way nor another. (We cling only to Christ as he lives in any kind of way.) For all else, we grasp neither at being rich nor being poor. Clutching desperately neither to being sick (some actually do) nor to being healthy.

It is about being free to choose Christ among a thousand saviors striving for our attention. Not to be fixing on reality and truth as we think they ought to be but on what Reality and Truth actually are.

Contemplate the Trinity gazing down on the earth, advises Ignatius. Meditate on the Nativity, the flight to Egypt, the woman at the well, Christ in the garden. Go, do this, work the exercises. A practice.

And so we practice. We meditate on the Call of the King. "If we give consideration to such a call from a temporal king to his subjects, how much more worthy of our consideration it is to gaze upon Christ our Lord? . . ."

Shall we follow such a one? First kiss, last breath, blue bottle flies, pinwheel in a flowerbox. The holy wandering *bodhisattva* shows up, she practices. She does not work up a lather over all the whys and reasons. She takes up. Slows the breath, shuts the eyes. Contemplates the wiping of feet with long hair and confessing tears. Kneels before the cardboard box and meditates on the picture of Michael—maybe he is gathering up strength to throw Satan down from heaven. A practice.

And for a seeker trying to pray but feeling no Presence at all? Any spiritual guide worth her salt advises such a one to pray as if there is Presence. To stand and act as if Christ actually exists. To fake a belief there is a God. And to see if, eventually, something starts to happen; to numbly take the small round host whenever he can and maybe find out one day it does, yes, it does speak.

Psychologists suggest the same to patients mired in their mental depths. Do things, act from what you value, pretend it matters, whether you are feeling it or not. Thoughts and emotions can shift, even a little. A path clears, a door opens a crack.

The seeker thinks he can hardly bear the crammed-in weight of all the human history Christ bears, and nevertheless, nevertheless he takes up. He volunteers to float along the line outside the soup kitchen, awkwardly striking up conversations. He reads scripture, takes up de Caussade, prays for a minute and then another. He says words he might never say, *yes, they are cute*, and, over time, becomes someone who tosses off those gracious descriptions without a thought, doing more for the bakers around him than he could ever imagine.

Root, Grunt, Skitter

Y OU'D RATHER TALK about the pigs.
It is not the ecclesiology of the heroic Jesuit mission you ultimately want to study and decipher, its prayers, devotions, and disciplines. It is the pigs—the pigs who simultaneously live in *samsara* and *nirvana*, immersed in the conventional and the ultimate, ignorant, enlightened pigs in their makeshift pen.

Pigs who, when they hear you coming, arise with a start, like soldiers caught sleeping, and scramble up and want food because that is what they always want. Five or fifty pigs with hard black bristly hair, under the shelter of eight brown boards.

The pigs and their bold self-proclamation: pig is what I am. I pig here. My grunts are the sweet lullaby for all the confused things of the earth. I am of such singular purpose as to be a tonic to those who think too much, who wonder at the divinity above and what he does or does not, and why so and why not, whence the evil and whence the good. I am such tonic because I, pig, know what I am about and what the god above is about. And in my root grunt skitter to my feet on the wooden planks as a slop bucket sweeps majestically toward me; in this I glorify all who share my purpose. And all do share my purpose: simply to receive the rinds, bones, peels, cores, and ten thousand other wonders of this world. But others. Others could stand to learn a lot from me. I eat. I love. I finish. I want to eat more.

I am in the grip of a certainty that things will be okay, that food will come from a bucket or from above, that the sun will rise and life matters and all the doubts of the world about the presence of Presence are really things to be grunted over quickly and then move on and just practice the sublime eating of things.

Trudy Is a Girl's Name

A T THE COFFEE SHOP where I write this, a man has popped in and given a box of chocolates to the counter girl. "You remembered!" she says. After he leaves, she tells me he is a customer and always brings her chocolates, and that tomorrow is her birthday.

His energy is not courting, seducing. There are no hooks in his present. It is just the simple gift of a grateful regular.

Why does a good God let us suffer? My childhood home is putty green. Why is the world saturated with evil? Rafa has won the French Open twelve times, and it's getting ridiculous. Why so much human pain? Adam and I caught semi-wild horses and rode them in the gathering Wyoming dusk. And vicious natural disaster? Dirt is granular. And terror? Spell arpeggio. Whence brutal crime? Peony Park was in Omaha and I rarely went. Where was the Prince of Peace when they delivered us unto Iraq? The church bell chimed ten. How could the towering might of God have failed to head off black sites and Abu Ghraib, the insanity of Meow Mix, the dogs, the hoods, the wires and the men stuffed in a small box, and the heads smashed against a wall, and rectal rehydration, and no sleep on day 2, day 5, day 12, day 19, no sleep and the water and the board and the way those two elemental things put together become a new kind of thing for rending a man apart. Why? A group of pigeons is called a clatter. Why does God let some minds go to soup while others soar? Everyone has a throat. Why do all those kids wind up in jail? There is no such thing as a clatter of pigeons. How could God birth us into this world and then just as quickly take us out? When I eat a bagel, I compare it with other bagels. Why the poisoning fog of depression? A flue is the throat of the chimney. Why did Christ have to die for our sins? Lickety split is fun to say. Who crashed the plane? The makers or the flyers, or the Creator of makers and flyers? Betty Botter bought some butter but she said this butter's bitter. How did we get to be so fundamentally broken? Something should be called a clatter. Whence the good deeds that go not unpunished? There's no I in team. Whence El Mozote? Trudy is a girl's name and a great one. Do you know why your father left? I mean, you know why he left, but in a larger kind of way, what made it all take place that there was the situation that met with the time that met with the place that joined with the woman that coincided with the color of your wallpaper, and the slant of your gutter, and the Camels he smoked, and the paving stones in your yard, and whoever was president at the time and whoever was chairman of the Joint Chiefs of Staff, and which wooden roller coasters that don't loop around were out of service, in which amusement parks in which seaside towns, and what shade of blue rode over the neighborhood that day, and what shade rode over every other neighborhood in every other place that day, and in general, the kind of guy he was that he would leave? Why? A man in a non-grasping way brings chocolates to the counter girl.

General Motors

A RE WE STILL not satisfied? All this and does it still not fully address the cosmic question of suffering? Every time we have it, something else cuts it down at the knees, no? What shall I tell you?

Perhaps this can be deftly handled once and for all by my decisive grad school paper on the Book of Job.

After his servants, his livestock, his sons and daughters were all annihilated, Job still reached out to the Lord. He prayed. Job's suffering teaches us to pray to God. It also chases us straight into the arms of God's people, finally realizing we need each other:

> "Is not man's life on earth a drudgery?" declares Job. "Are not his days like those of a hireling? He is a slave who longs for the shade, a hireling who waits for his wages." In this we have the

first traces of a man reconciling his relationship with the divine. Job radically and clearly gives voice to his suffering.

Job continues his anguished cry.

"Perish the day on which I was born, the night when they said, 'The child is a boy!' Let that day be darkness: let not God above call for it, nor light shine upon it!" In this line, and the whole speech that follows, we see Job telling the world what is going on: calling out his pain, his anguish, his frustration, his cosmic predicament. In this, he rinses out his angers and fears. He offers a kind of tormented prayer to God. He claims the full scope of his limited, confusing human condition. How critical this is!

"Excellent points. Well-stated! A fine close reading of the text."

Acknowledge your utter humanity. Give it all to God. Now you can really begin to pray. You do not end suffering. You end suffering by dealing with suffering. Need we say it again?

It is a mystery, yes, pain and tragedy attends it all. It speaks to the unbearable mystery of God in the universe, all of our time in *samsara*. But in the face of suffering, we may, if we choose, draw nearer to our God. We tell the story until we can affix our painful stories to the

Almighty, to the Larger-than-Hurt. Philip, whose heart I am in and the remnant of El Mozote and the kids to whom things were done: yes, it may be they are all led closer to God. "To you I call, O Lord, my Rock; do not turn a deaf ear to me." The psalmist knew what Job knows: that sometimes all you can do is cry out in your pain.

"To behold divine mysteries," says de Caussade, "it is necessary to shut the eyes to what is external, and to cease to reason." Don't dare use the word God. Gød will do just fine.

There you have it, one more time. Now let's wrap this up and move on. Pray. Confront suffering. Refuse the steep rent of an exhausted mind and just exist. God is there.

Does that make anyone feel a lot better? Does it help us all to veer away from the blades of exquisite pain? *You can confront your suffering and be serene and draw close to God. I'd rather have my fiancé back. Just one solitary human person re-formed from the ashes of Manhattan and placed back on my front stoop. Is that too much to ask? Can I hightail out of the dark soul into the light of something wrong called pure elation?*

Darnell, age eleven, in for first-degree sexual misconduct. He tells me that some girls played a game on him and got him kicked out of the projects. He informs me the devil threw a blanket over him. Back in JDC. In the state pen. In federal. Chaplain them all you want, novice. Long talks and exhortations and bible passages and games of Hearts and your own solitary prayer and still, every last one.

Darnell tells me about his bad dreams, a looming dead grandfather angry at him for doing wrong things. Darnell used to thieve. One day, he read in the Bible, "Don't steal." He rubbed his eyes. "Is that really in there?" He read again, fell asleep, had another bad dream, and then felt he was saved. He was saved! Later, another boy hurt his friend, and Darnell attacked him. He started hitting the other boy, then remembered that the Bible said, "Don't do it." Darnell took the boy's switchblade, flicked it and was about to cut his own wrists. Then he heard a voice saying, "Don't do it."

Darnell goes on: "God wants you to swim. If you drown, God saves you. But then God throws you out again, and says come here, swim to me. But the devil pulls you under."

At the end of all this tumbling complicated narrative, he boils things down to what is essential: "Does God then reach out to you to help you swim or does he let you drown?"

Well, which one is it?

They will all be back.

Clap harder, children, clap harder! Tinkerbell might awaken! Bad things might not have happened if people were only following God. Dives and his brothers might have avoided the eternal fire if they had listened to Moses and the prophets. If only journalists and Christians, organizers and peacemakers and politicians were more alert and courageous, we might have headed off Iraq. Iraq and what it brought, blast waves that shear tissue, rupture the testicles, explode the eye; shrapnel that sends bone and muscle flying and lifts a spine from its back; and by now, as of this writing two hundred thousand civilians gone and counting and Daniel Berrigan would not in his old age have had to traffic in such heartbreak.

While the world still tries to get a grip on God, remove barriers to Christ, and find the perfect pitch between conventional reality and ultimate reality and claim whole-heartedly its sorrowful condition, there are—did we say this already?—just a lot of intensely disturbing things that go on down here and never seem to end. Once more we name it, for what else is there to name?

A woman named Jen Gann tells the world that which no human mother is allowed to say: that she loves her young child fiercely, more than anything else on earth, but had she known while she was pregnant that he was afflicted with cystic fibrosis and would suffer as terribly as he does, and would need the kind of hyper-intensive care he does, and would die as young as he probably will, had she known all that, she would have had an abortion. She would have stopped this before it began.

And what kind of existence is this where a woman must bear in one heart and mind such agonizing, mind-shaking, and impossible contradictions? The most distressing but real rendering of non-contradiction you can get?

Is she a sheer monster, reading infanticide back into her history? A marker of a callous, godless age? Or just more terribly honest than any mother in those circumstances who, if even for a bare moment, thinks the same way? Nothing can legislate where the mind goes.

And if Jen Gann's child enters the world with this condition thirty years from now when a cure for cystic fibrosis has arisen out of some miraculous microscope, she won't even have to consider such a choice, and there is just really no sense. And God is immovable, and men, women, and children sit immovable, while the waters rise over their heads.

I learned one supreme and vital thing in my years of theology and philosophy studies. I discovered you can make a case for pretty much anything. You enter the library and browse the magazines and check out the bulletin board and use the bathroom and finally look for the card catalog and remember, yet again, there are no card catalogs anymore, so you go to the WorldCat database and find your book and confront the lordly grad school librarian, who undergoes what appears to be great suffering to break up whatever he was doing to perform his job on your behalf, and then you sit in a library carrel and then your desk at home and then a coffee shop and then back to your desk and scour the internet for Northern California shark attacks, and organize your thoughts and finally write your paper and make your case. And when you are done, a case has been made.

A very fine, smart-looking, well-argued case can be made for just about anything. You can make a case using Job, Asanga, Jean-Pierre de Caussade, or Dionysus the Areopagite for why there is suffering, or why we can't even talk about suffering, or how God works in suffering, or anything you please.

But no matter what theology or spirituality or philosophy tells us, it keeps happening. People keep getting born straight into it. Buildings keep falling, collapsing over asset managers in Manhattan or garment workers in Bangladesh. And other towers don't move an inch. Not a hair. Writes the poet Katie Ford:

> Where's it gone? God of my childhood,
> with your attendant monstrosities,
> have a little warmth on me, bent and frozen.

Most thoughtful priests in the sanctuary today will indicate, in one way or another, that the God of the New Testament is different from the God of the Old Testament. We have a more enlightened God. We know God better than they knew God. God does not rip into the world with such vengeance. We have Jesus, we have love—a love more profound than that prescribed by the Law.

But rarely will anyone point out that God is still making us with such tender skin! Pound for pound, the most vulnerable epidermis of any creature out there. And still, via secondary causes, he grows a world of sharp edges, high cliffs, vicious hurricanes, unrelenting plagues, and handy tempting raw materials for any weapon large or small. A world that takes our skin to the woodshed again, again, and again.

General Motors was like this. Don't laugh. I think it's true. Surely GM meant no evil when they built their mid-century cars with such sharp edges and wicked points that ended up maiming, let alone killing scores of people who got in wrecks. They were not out to slice anyone up. But eventually, a young lawyer who used to hitchhike the country and saw these horrific accidents, showed up and pointed out to them the exact nature of their wrongs.

Here is the difference. GM started making their cars safer.

To save lives, save face, redeem the company? For sheer profit's sake?

Who cares? They changed up their little piece of the world that cut people down so viciously.

But God hasn't stopped. God makes humans so delicate, and then creates a mind so sharp and vast it is able to build things that can rip apart that skin like tissue paper. We know this. We tell God this all the time. The Spirit that flows through all things keeps creating more of us, and God, hands tied behind his back, is not complicit?

The God who "allows" this all to continue cannot be brought to trial with the rest of corrupt humanity?

Augustine from the *Enchiridion*: "Since God is the highest good he would not allow any evil to exist in his works unless His omnipotence and goodness were such as to bring good even out of evil."

Carmelo after the death of Kobe Bryant: "This will never make sense to me." Nevertheless, "I know I'm not supposed to question GOD's Will. I know GOD doesn't make mistakes."

Or Aquinas, who is so hopeful about the state of the world, the goodness residing in all things! "Every creature of God is good; and God is the greatest good. Therefore every being is good."

Aquinas goes on in his listing of good things as related to our earthly lives: "Goodness is that which all things desire." And "everything seeks after its own perfection," and "Because of this, all desired perfections flow from Him as the first cause."

God wills all things to the good—uses our sorrows and evils to lead to something better. "It belongs to the great power of God that he acts immediately in all things. Hence nothing is distant from Him, as if it could be without God in itself."

Who doesn't love thinking like this in a world of no sense? Aquinas as a calm dad at the wheel telling us that everything is going to be all right in the moment we are driving off the cliff. "This is part of the infinite goodness of God that he should allow evil to exist and out of it produce good." Thank you, Pop!

Yes, God's goodness is far bigger than any badness out there. Evil can produce good. *This beating I am giving you, sayeth the Lord. This evil I am letting happen;*

allowing you to endure; giving you free will to dish out on someone else. It is all for your own good. There is something better ahead. In this world or the next.

So, get there, says God, helpfully. *Get to belief, to recognizing that it is all for you.*

[Pause]

Go on, Faint of Heart and Crushed with Pain, go. What are you waiting for? Why aren't you going?

REMEMBER THE NOVICE who talked about the way his people collect crops? They eat the plant, and then they have to go, and they go in the forest, anywhere they please, and the plant grows all over again because there are seeds in their stool.

A Dark-Lit Chapel

A MAN SAT DOWN in a small chapel on a Wednesday at noon and told a spirituality gathering about all the pain and suffering he had in his life—it was a lot, the details escape me, but it was brutal and precise, a cross dropped in its hole, his body jarred inhumanly—and then he said he knows that all his suffering was God's will for him.

He spoke in a slowly coming-to-terms way, with clear gentle hesitation, with assured clean logic. No hint of evangelism, no breath of apologetics. God willed all my suffering. The faintest smile on his lips that was not a smile, not the smug tidying up of religion, just him talking as his mouth goes into a one-quarter grin, I guess, when he talks.

Or him being kind of amazed at his life, I can't believe I am going to say this, but God willed all this hardship into my life—the things I brought on myself and what was brought on me. I know this because I have gone to the depths, the deepest of black sites, and have been released. I have found something very good I would not have found otherwise. "What is hell?" asks Father Zossima in *The Brothers Karamazov*. Hell, for Zossima, is "the suffering of being no longer able to love." I could not love, declares our featured speaker, and now I can. It must be, then, God.

It was the most blatantly—what word, what word? Securing? No. Enfolding? No. Frightening? No, no—it was most blatantly—the thing you wanted somehow to hear and not hear—over and over again, for every moment of the rest of your life. His afflictions had cast him down eye-level with other afflicted people, and now that he knew what it was like, he could finally be useful to them.

It was in a small room—wood paneling, stone floor—a tiny perfect chapel, lit but still dark, at a non-religious spirituality conference, and he sat at the front on a wood chair with blond thatching and told us what was the what.

The worst thing you ever heard. God caused it all. The theology of his life, his voice, a tone, a certainty of experience deeper than any words of the *Summa Theologiae*. A theology of pauses, of words edging through truth, a slow train of letters forming the unthinkable: *Deus vult*. God wills it. A singular dogma of the breath slowly seeping into a chapel turned secular and instantly crammed with as much religion as you ever felt in your life.

A theodicy of the ghost of a smile that is not a smile but just awe at himself and the One who freed him to be himself; a theology of the way his skin was beneath his clothes, and how his feet filled his shoes, and blood swept through his veins; a sermon without persuasion, as if he was just saying it for himself and we just happened to be there. A theology of quiet words picked carefully in a lower register in a crowded chapel on Wednesday. It was all God's will.

He told us and we nodded and were not shocked because everyone at this conference was a bit desperate for just such type of words and were willing to take whatever we could get.

Aquinas on the mystery of God's presence in suffering and evil makes no sense, nor John of the Cross, Augustine, Jean-Luc Marion, Abraham, nor this guy in this chapel. But this guy made no sense more beautifully than any of them.

The blue messenger bag tucked awkwardly beneath my chair, black shoes with sharp aggressive soles, me feeling oh so ridiculous and nailed down in the seat. I want what you have; I want to run a thousand miles from what you have.

And just how can this be? A theory: God so wants to be with you that he will go anywhere you go—even into the teeth of the beast of suffering and even if by doing so it appears that he is causing your affliction. And thus, the merest ounce of the Lord that jumped on the lever of pain that was going to come at you anyway actually caused it to tip. God didn't mean to tilt the lever of suffering, he just wanted to be there, but it did go down because he got there first before suffering got there because he always gets to places first because he is God.

And so it seems the unintended consequences of God's excessive love caused the scales of cosmic hurt to fall and you to fall into great distress, to get your moth wings charred black and gone.

The tiny perfect dark chapel and the guy who was transformed into a terror called no love and now he believes God did this to him, and he wasn't telling us what God does to you, just to him. God brought down the beam.

And all the smart things we might say to soften the blow of such horrific words as God caused my suffering. Pinpoint analysis. Academic throat-clearing. Dissecting the religio-historical daisy chain of such noontime chapel pronouncements.

No. Professor DiStefano has you by the lapels: Cut it out. Quit analyzing the pericope he just chanted. Leave off thieving this scripture of its meaning and just behold his faint smile and the tone of his voice, feel the heart of him and your own heart. Cast out Van Seters and all his minions and just listen and be in awe.

The God who jumps on the shovel just as Satan digs into the flesh, the God who sharpens the hornet's stinger just as it pierces the skin so that God's fingerprints can be upon it, so he can go where we go.

Our towers had crashed, our antennae were down, and we were lost in the dark with the gutty team with the bright sunshine outside, the wood paneling, the close-knit gang of us conference-goers, the bundled-up happy clutch of us, a few of us spent, on the canvas, but all of us in it—in it to win it, dammit. The critical mass of us receiving generalized spirituality that turned the church fathers on their head and made rabbinic midrash look like a nursery rhyme.

His life was not perfect, but it was pretty much okay. Which for him, considering everything, meant it was extraordinarily good. He was closer to God. He fell for the joke—went through a very bad time, was depleted by God, and finally gave up and let God clean him out utterly, strip him to the bone. And he surrendered again and again, becoming something new. What the spirit emptied the spirit filled back up. His resurrection appeared to be worth all the unspeakable pain.

That's his experience anyway. Can you really argue with someone's experience? There is no hope for these children? Who knows about hope?

O Death

GOD WILLED HIS SUFFERING. It still pelts the mind just to say it. As God willed Philip's condition? As God pulled Cade, the wrestler, into heaven, to join Brandon and Carrie and his ever-mounting collection of high school all-stars? As God took down El Salvador and Iraq and sprinkled on a newborn the magic dust of a near-criminal disease that would turn a mother completely inside out? As God strung along all those boys into JDC?

As God occasioned the death of that healthy charming priest where his niece at the wake read, "O death, where is your victory? O death, where is your sting?" God's will was the unmoved mover of that?

The passage was recited in a voice that was, it seemed, trying to keep from breaking; a voice that issued a threat, a monotone and rapid threat to death, O death, where is thy victory: *Is that all you got, death?* But you could tell she didn't really believe it.

The priest had been in great shape, of course, and then suddenly his heart, and suddenly she is reading with no emotion, flat and fast: let's just get this over with and move on to the part where this isn't true, where it's all a big joke on her.

He was a priest on a Lakota reservation and good at being that and was in his fifties with no hint of mortality anywhere. He loved poetry and would find you in the house and read a poem to you. Then he would pause and look at you and then basically leave. It was always pretty much one of the best, or maybe just strangest, poetry readings you'd ever been to. He wore a nylon jacket that read "Thorpes." This is not about him.

O death. I thought it was invented by Appalachian songwriters. I had known it comes from Paul, but I thought it was something so iconic and archaic and southern mountain tragic it was not really read at church anymore because being so co-opted by gravel-voiced banjo-strumming holler and stream culture, it was excised from the canon. O death, where is thy victory? O death, where is thy sting?

The fact we die, went the theology of Christ's time, is a result of our sin. Yet, declared Paul, the death and resurrection of Christ conquered sin, so that ultimately death has no power over us. On the last day, death will be rendered helpless for we will all be raised from it, and I don't even believe this thing that I am reading at the wake, I am just reading because I am the niece. (Who knows what she was actually thinking?)

And she reads. And you could barely place a needle in the space between her tone and the words she recites. It is unpleasant that I am here. This is not good, and death, you have nothing on me and it is a practice.

It is meant as a taunt—a child scoffing at another child. That's the best you can do? Really? No sting? No victory? I thought you were so much more! You glance off me, death, like a pebble off a brick wall, a bee sting on a whale. You are nothing. Jesus is our victory. When I see you, death and sin and evil, I just say, with a hearty Full Gospel Holiness twang: *God's got this*.

And yet it comes to pass, someone you love dies young and the brassy reading becomes a taunt of ourselves. Where is death's sting? Anyone in the dark on this one? Come close. *It's right here*. It has pierced my entire body, it has claimed all my territory. Your sting has taken me to the floor, your victory is total and complete. Because I can only see darkly through conventional reality, and your sting, O death, has brought me down.

The question posed to death is not ironic when you are cycling through *samsara*, caught up in real life. It is an indictment. Death, you are destroying me. I feel the sting of your sting of your sting pummeling me into the ground.

If I were traveling firm and straight along the Eightfold Path, just this side of enlightenment, I could look down and laugh at this. I know the plan! The Lord conquers death, you fool. Death, you have no power. I have put on the armor of Christ. The belt around my waist is Cade's memorial T-shirt, and you cannot touch me.

But as I am, a normal person alive . . . no, I can't bear the exposed nerve of this savior and the suffering he allows.

And thus the niece's voice for the span of one wake reading sums up all of apophaticism, all of two realities, all of Christian mysticism and spirituality, everything we hope for and everything we shudder to think on, the universe in a teardrop: Death is crushing me. Death has nothing on me.

Before me a word of love that I fully believe and in this moment fully disbelieve but am reading anyway, a practice. Because, if I say it enough times, maybe the message will drop into my blood until it courses through me entire. I go through the motions of belief until the motions go through me.

THE KNOWLEDGE is over there. We are tethered to that knowledge. We know it is there—the reasons for suffering. They have told us the knowledge exists. It has been spoken in our ears, written on our parchment. God's presence, God's love, the hope for the glorious beyond, conforming ourselves to Christ's blank face or to the splintered wood of the cross when we suffer. It has all been laid out.

But that knowledge exists in a different country, and Lord knows we don't live there. That place on the map is far off, distant seas away, and we don't have residency, and can barely make it out in the gray skies. The claim, "God willed my suffering" or "God uses evil to bring out the good," that it's all God's plan, that God only gives us what we can handle—any words that attempt to explain the way God works in human suffering—is a bad translation of a language that hasn't even been invented yet.

Still, we say things, do what we can, pluck out the arrow, let it be plucked.

Candle

I DON'T THINK I'LL MENTION Easter, because we know, no? Easter, you could say, has mentioned us, claimed what is weak in our weak; hijacked what is afraid in our fear. You don't even have to think on the words, no, you don't. I am on the number 2 train riding to Easter. So mundane, this day, so obvious. It happens every year! And they turned back from Emmaus, and told the others. John stayed on the threshold and looked in.

The words of resurrection capture us, pull us like a boy with some stubborn pony, haul us into their contours and rhythms, their vowels and consonants. Peter kneels and looks at the burial cloths, and the stubborn beast of us kneels down with him, looking in and going away amazed. I am on the train to an Easter vigil, at a church for, of all people, actors.

And less amazed maybe at Christ gone because we know he is gone. But amazed more at ourselves, that this thing works—we Jesuits at least, chaste, obedient, sent into every kind of thing and it works; sometimes on a bare edge, the substance and heft of a rope made of grass, this life, vowed religious, single beds, but any life in a cosmic sense is single bed and here we are, all of us, the words wrap us up in their burial clothes, we die with Christ, but the story is not over because when what's true is killed, it becomes its own spring which like any given bulb at the appointed time in the loamy soil of daylight will rise again and something new is coming. I have seen faintly smiling miracles in dark-lit spaces everywhere.

And if I told you I was convinced that the damaged man screaming and dancing in my train car and just taken away by cops would be made a little better because it was Holy Saturday, and in a few minutes, I would stand with lit wick before the Paschal candle and the smoke and light of that candle would trail all the way down the street to a sidewalk grate to the train line to his soul walled up in some police station or mental ward, I would be lying. I am not convinced of it. He still suffers, he is still a wreck. Maybe he always will be.

If he had no deep imprint of love before the age of two, as they say, it was all settled for him. Like maybe it was settled at age two for those boys in the Minneapolis JDC, no deep imprint, and nevertheless, God does find himself here, nowhere but here. Divinity pinned like a moth into deep reality; in small faces in jail or their older version on a train, getting hauled away by cops, but maybe it isn't finished. You go up to the lectern, turn open the page, eyes sweep across the wake, no emotion, tempted to reify, maybe someone will take care of this guy, seared with repudiation, standing there anyway, speaking with no sense, maybe it's on us, speaking because the story is not over, O death, where is...where is...where is thy sting? Did you know, O death, that, in your dark waste, there are always seeds?